Barnsley Libraries

CENT

Sargeant Sergeant

Also by Peter Knowles

Once Upon a Time in the Army

Club Seventy Seven

Sargeant Sergeant
by
Peter Knowles

Sargeant Sergeant

The original erotic/unabridged version of the book Once Upon A Time in the Army

Copyright 2010 © Peter Knowles

ISBN: 978-1-4457-7466-4

Erotic Fiction

Sargeant Sergeant

1966

Once upon a time outside the art college with some of my fellow students, Willie Wanker, Billy Blow Job, Tosser and me, John Thomas Sargeant, aka 'The Sarge'.

The reason we were outside and not inside where we should have been is this, we had all just been expelled from the college for painting a nude, well that's not exactly true, yes the girl was nude and yes she did have paint on her, I thought we were being very artistic but the teachers had other ideas.

We sound like a right bunch of perverts, but I assure you we were all red blooded males with a very healthy interest in girls, painted or otherwise.

Willie suddenly announced he was going to join the army, after a lot of piss taking by the rest of us he bet us twenty quid apiece that we hadn't got the guts to do the same.

Now twenty quid was a lot of money in those days and like idiots we took the wager without thinking of the consequences, so off we went to the recruiting office.

The recruiting Sergeant greeted us with a hand shake.

"Come in lads, you want to join the army do you".

That was the first and last time a Sergeant ever shook my hand.

"What's your name lad?" he asked, looking me straight in the eye.

"John Thomas Sargeant, err Sergeant" I spluttered.

"Sargeant Sergeant" he chuckled to himself sitting back down at his desk.

The Corporal at the other desk was giggling like a big daft tart, what did I say that was so funny?

Anyway he gave us all the usual crap about how good life was in the army, we did a sort of entrance test thingy, you know the sort of thing knocking square pegs into round holes, all that we had to do now was to pass the medical.

A few weeks later I received a letter saying I'd passed the entrance test and the medical and would I go back to the recruiting office to be signed up.

Thinking Billy and Tosser must have got the same letter, I went and signed on the dotted line and became a soldier.

Later that same day I met up with Billy and Tosser, they had also received a letter like I had, but Billy was only seventeen and needed his parent's permission to join up and they wouldn't give it to him, Tosser had failed his medical because there something wrong with his tackle, too much bloody wanking that was his problem and Willie had now changed his mind about joining so that just left me.

'Thanks Guys'.

I must admit I thought about changing my mind but I'd already had and spent the wages the army paid me on the day I signed up, I had the travel warrant to York in my pocket and my suitcase was already packed.
Come to think of it, I never did get my twenty quid off Willie.....
The Wanker.

Queen Elizabeth's Bollocks

There I was, suitcase in hand on my way to York, Queen Elizabeth's Bollocks, Strensell York to be exact.
I never could pronounce the word 'Barracks' and still can't to this day, in my Yorkshire accent it always comes out as 'Ballacks'.

On the train I met a lad who had also just joined up and was on his way to York, his name was Arnold Sidebottom, he seemed a bit gay to me, with a name like Sidebottom what do you expect and in true army fashion he got nicknamed 'Justin'. I wasn't too keen on him, but for the time being travelling with him was better than being on my own, little did I know at the time that I would spend most of my army career with him.

On arrival at York we had to report to the guard room, by now there were quite a few of us, all new recruits, or 'Red Arses' as we were later to be known, I joined the queue outside and we were summoned in one by one. "Next", bellowed a voice from within. I stepped through the door.
"Name?" shouted a burly Corporal through the sliding glass window that looked just like the serving hatch of our local off licence, I nearly ordered two bottles of beer and a bag of crisps.
"Name?" shouted the Corporal again, "Don't yer know yer fukin name or what".
"Orr what" I stammered.
"Fuck me" says the Corporal, "Your fuckin name, what is it?"
"Errrr, John Thomas Sargeant".
"I'm not a Sergeant" said the Corporal
"No my name is John Thomas Sargeant" I said, trying to correct him.
"John Thomas Sargeant, what?" he demanded.
"John Thomas Sargeant, Corporal" I shouted back, he seemed to like being shouted at.
"That's better and stand to attention when an NCO speaks to you" said the Corporal, trying not to laugh.
What was so funny about my name? I thought, 'If you think that's funny,

wait until Justin comes in next'.

Another NCO came and stood next to him.

"Having a problem, Corporal?" he asked.

"No Sir just processing young John Thomas Sargeant, nearly done Sir" said the Corporal standing to attention.

"John Thomas Sargeant eh" said the Sergeant Major, "I've just read a book about you" he said, chuckling and walking away.

"OK lad, wait outside" said the Corporal, "Next".

Waiting outside it suddenly dawned on me what they thought was funny, I am now Private Sargeant. I kept saying it to myself over and over again, 'hope I never get promoted to the rank of Sergeant and I must get hold of a copy of that book he was on about'.

After everyone had been in the guardroom we were shown to a barrack room, told to leave our suitcases and follow the NCO to the stores to get our kit. With the kit came an inventory sheet and we were told to check the sheet against the kit to make sure nothing was missing, because any lost kit had to be paid for.

Now everything in the army is backwards, so reading the inventory went something like this, for example.

You don't get 'one pair of trousers', you get 'trousers pair one'. 'Boots DMS pairs two', and so on. Now what confused me was the 'housewife one', what the hell is a 'housewife one', she's my father's wife my mother, isn't she, or did the army have a supply of unwanted married mother's that they issued to every soldier.

We should be so lucky, convinced I hadn't got mine, I asked the NCO, he looked through my kit and said "Yep, it's there". He hadn't actually pointed to it or touched it so not wanting to look a prat, I just said "Oh yea, there it is". But I still didn't know what my housewife was. Now Justin did, well he would wouldn't he, he picked it up, handed it to me and I opened it.

"Oh no it's a bleeding sewing kit" does this mean I have to do my own mending.

I am not going to go into the details of army training, spit and polish, room inspections, kit inspections, locker inspections, drill and all the other pointless tasks, we all know that the job of the army to beat you down and then build you back up into a lean mean fighting machine. That's not what this book is about and there are plenty of 'How we won the war books' on the market, so the last thing anyone needs is another.

So let me introduce you to the lads, we were '3' Section '5' Platoon, Quebec Company, there were ten of us in our room, starting from the left side near the door has you entered the room there was Paul Smith with two F's, aka 'Smudge', next to him was a small weedy little kid called Peter, I can't remember his surname, but I do recall it was something that sounded like the name of a well known brand of washing powder so we called him 'Suds', next came a lad from Scotland called Angus McCoatup or something like that, he got nicknamed 'Rob' after Rob Roy, then Arnold came ,it's hard to give someone called Sidebottom a nickname so like I said earlier, we called him 'Justin', and in the bottom corner was Tom Brown, aka 'Schooldays'. On the right hand side of the room was 'Midnight' a West Indian lad, I can't remember his name and I probably couldn't pronounce it anyway, then there was Alan Murphy, aka 'Spud', followed by another Scottish lad called Stuart Wales, a strange name for a scot so we called him 'Taffy', then came Selwyn Jones, now he should have been 'Taffy' with a good old welsh name like that, but no he got called 'Gapper' because his front teeth were missing and anyway he came from Sheffield not Wales, and in the bottom corner was yours truly, me.

Our NCO's were Lance Corporal 'Jacko' Jackson, Corporal 'Bren' Gunn, Sergeant 'Nosey' Parker and the platoon commander was a 2nd Lieutenant Ponsonby, but they weren't classed as one of the lads, they just thought they were in charge.

Now Lt Ponsonby was the very first army officer I had ever met, what a twit with his posh voice and his 'Follow me chaps' attitude. Follow him I wouldn't follow him to the shit house never mind into battle.

Once during training we were in some woods in the middle of the night, pitch black it was, you couldn't see 'Midnight' in front of your face, unless he smiled at you.

Ponsonby was explaining about staying on the light coloured ground and not walking on the dark ground as it could be a ditch.

"Follow me chaps" he says, turns, then promptly disappears, had he suddenly been abducted by aliens had some unseen enemy taken him as hostage, walking gingerly up to where he had disappeared we heard him say,

"Don't come down here chaps, there's a hole"

"No fuckin kidding" said Smudge, up to that point we had all kept our composure and stifled the urge to laugh, that was it the moment had gone and we all fell about laughing.

Cpl Gunn came running through the blackness towards us, Schooldays stuck his leg out and Bren Gunn went arse over tit straight down the hole on top of poor Poncey.

"Ouch! Bastard" yells Bren, from the hole.

"Get off me Corporal Gunn" demanded Poncey.

"Sorry sir, tripped and fell sir, sorry" said Bren.

He really did think he had tripped it was only afterwards that Schooldays admitted to us that he had stuck his leg out and tripped him on purpose.

"Help us out Sargeant" said Bren looking up from the hole.

'Sergeant, Nosey Parker's not here' I thought.

Oh, Sargeant, me, "Gather round lads, come on give us a hand here" I shouted.

Most of the lads were still creased up with laughter and were of no bloody use at all. I pulled Bren clear of the hole and Justin pulled poncey clear, he started to brush him down, to dust the muck off him, in reality I think Justin just wanted to touch.

"Get off me Sidebottom" shrieked Poncey.

"Haven't touched your bottom" mumbled Justin walking away, looking a little rejected.

"Going back to the mess corporal to get cleaned up, see to the chaps" said Poncey.

"Right Sir" said Bren.

What kind of army was this, stop the war, the officer got dirty and went back to the mess.

"OK you set of wankers" shouted Bren

"Now he's gone let's get one thing straight, you do not laugh at your platoon commander, even if he is a prat".

He then burst into laughter and set us all off again.

"Wakey Wakey Rise and Shine you red arses, hands off your cocks and onto your socks" screamed Sgt Parker bursting into the barrack room and banging the hell out of a metal bin lid with his pace stick.

"What the fuck" we all said in unison.

"Come on, out of them sweaty pits you idol fuckin lot it's rifle range today, let's see if you can fuckin kill each other" announced Nosey.

"Kill you, yer noisey twat" moaned Schooldays.

"I heard that Brown, if yer kill me I'll come back n bloody haunt yer you fukin o'rrable little towrag" Nosey shouted back has he left the room.

We could still hear him bellowing in the distance and going through the same ritual in all the other rooms.

We had been on the rifle range about an hour, when Captain Montford aka 'Monty' the camp adjutant, strolls up.

Nosey Parker snaps to attention. "Attention" he commands.

Now we are lying on the ground rifles in hand on the firing range how the bloody hell do you lay to attention?

"Morning Sir" says Nosey, and salutes him,

"Morning Sergeant Parker, just taking Cromwell for his morning walkies, what" replies Monty.

"Live firing sir, mind the dog" says Nosey.

"Yes, I will Sergeant, what" replies Monty,

"Come Cromwell, what" then off he strolls, Cromwell took no notice he never did, one word from Monty and the dog did has he pleased. Cromwell was a sort of sausage type dog but a bit bigger, he was about four feet long, a foot wide and the poor little bugger's legs were only about four inches long, he had the biggest cock on any dog you have ever seen, when he walked it dragged on the ground, not surprised he couldn't keep up with Monty. The lads called him Snowplough because of the tracks he left behind in the snow and the pile of snow he pushed along under his belly.

A short time later Monty returns. Nosey Parker salutes him again and once again we lie to attention on the ground.

"Have you seen my dog, what?" asks Monty.

"No sir not since you were here last" replies Nosey.

"There he is sir" said a voice from up the line of prone bodies on the ground.

"Where?" came back another voice.

"On the butts Sir" was the reply.

Now, for those of you who don't know what the 'Butts' are, they are the part of the range where the targets are.

We all looked down the range and sure enough there was Cromwell having a shit.

"Here Cromwell" shouted Monty.

Cromwell didn't take a blind bit of notice as usual.

"Here Cromwell there's a good boy, what" shouted Monty again, and again, and still Cromwell took no notice.

After a few more try's, everyone joined in with comments like "For fucks sake" and "Dozy bastard thing" but this was annoying Monty and Nosey Parker told us to "Shut it" or we would be on a charge.

Peace restored, Nosey Parker got on the field telephone and asked the lads in the butts to try and retrieve the dog, but Cromwell was having none of it.

"Here Cromwell" shouts Monty again, "There will be no peaches and cream for tea if you don't come now, what", and still Cromwell took no notice.

Now this is where Monty really lost the plot.

"Cromwell if you don't be a good boy and come here now I will order these boys to shoot you, what" he screamed at the dog. Ah! That worked, Cromwell looked towards us, then turned around pissed up one of the targets and proceeded to walk back along the top of the butts.

I remember thinking 'Why the fuck don't you walk down the range and get your own fuckin dog you lazy bastard it's only 500 yards'.

"Right boys shoot my dog" screamed Monty, who was by now bright red in the face with rage. Nosey Parker hurriedly walked down the back of the row of men still laid in the firing positions.

"Don't you fuckin dare" he commanded out of the corner of his mouth trying not to let Monty hear him.

"Shoot my dog" ordered Monty again.

Then we heard it, the sound of the 'Gimpy' being cocked. The 'Gimpy' is the 'General Purpose Machine Gun' or G.P.M.G. capable of firing about a 1,000 rounds a minute.

Nosey Parker set off in the direction of the machine gun but before he had chance to say anything.

Rat. Tat. Tat. Tat. Tat. Rat. Tat. Tat. Tat, too late.

Rob Roy who was manning the 'Gimpy' let off two bursts and poor old Cromwell disappeared in a cloud of dust.

There were bits of Cromwell all over the butts, we were sent with plastic bags to pick up what was left while Rob Roy was marched off the guard room under arrest and Monty just stood there saying "What, What, What" over and over again. Well he had given the order all Rob did was obey it.

That was his defence he says he never heard Nosey Parker tell him not to fire. When we got back to the barracks Rob's bed had gone and we never saw him again, we did hear he had been kicked out of the army.

As for Cromwell, he got a nice little grave behind the officer's mess and every now and again there were fresh flowers on it, put there we assume by Monty.

Now that just confirms my belief that the higher the rank in the army, the more stupid the person.

Nights in the barrack room were to say the least boring, we were meant to be bulling (cleaning) practicing weapons drill and such other delights, as I said meant to be, most of the time we were just laid about on our beds, that was until an NCO entered the building then it was amazing how busy you can look doing nothing.

One night Justin went off to the washroom for a shower, when he returned he had with him a large stick of Dobie soap which we used to clean clothes with, he had

fashioned it into a dildo about a foot long and really fat it had a flange, veins and looked just like the real thing, except it was bright yellow. Justin looking like the cat who got the cream was really pleased with his handy work or was it because he had been having fun with it in the shower.

He stood there wanking it. "Look" he said, "You can get a right lather up", the soap went all creamy in his hand,

"Oh, Oh, Oh, vinegar stroke" he groaned as if cuming for real then wearing only a towel he proceeded to dance around the room with the dildo between his legs flicking the soap suds everywhere.

At that moment 'Suds' walked into the room, also dress only in only a towel, had these two be in the shower together, no they can't have, could they. I know that none of the others, myself included, dare go near the shower room if Justin was in there, you just didn't know what he will do next, or was that my imagination running riot again.

Justin still running around see's Suds and makes a bee line straight for him, he grabs a hold of Suds towel and yanks it away leaving him bollock naked. Suds jumped onto his bed trying to get away but Justin jumped on top of him with the soap dildo still between his legs and thrusting away for all he was worth.

If Suds hadn't been wriggling so much I swear he would have been fucked, literally.

By now the whole room was cheering him on. Justin then jumped off Suds and whipped his own towel away to reveal the biggest erection you have ever seen.

"Look at that" he says, holding his cock in his hand. It was nearly as big as the soap dildo, now we know what he used for a model.

God I wish I had one like that" said Smudge.

"Play your cards right love and you can, I'm off for a wank" announces Justin and promptly sets off in the direction of the toilet block with his cock in one hand, a body building magazine and the soap dildo in the other.

"Needs some big black mamba" said Midnight holding his crotch and thrusting it towards Justin.

"And you too" replied Justin.

"Can we watch?" asked Spud.

"Kinky madam" said Justin, "Watch, you can take part if you like".

So was that it, had Justin finally come out.

I always knew he was bating for the other team.

Most nights there was something weird going on, more often than not one or more of the lads would be playing a practical joke of some sort.

After a few beers in the NAAFI, half pissed and giggling like little school girls. 'Midnight', 'Spud', 'Smudge' and I came back to the room.

The others were asleep.

"Shush" says Midnight putting his finger across his lips "Let's put one of them outside".

"They are in bed" said Spud,

"Yer, put one outside in his bed" said Midnight.

Being half pissed, this seemed like a good idea.

"How the hell, we going to do that"? I asked.

"Open the window" said Midnight, pointing at the door.

The windows in the barrack room were the big sash type, and a bed would easily fit through.

Smudge opened the window, in came a cold breeze of fresh air, this disturbed Schooldays in the end bed, he turned over and mumbled something incoherent, pulled his blankets up to his neck and went back to sleep, so we couldn't put him outside he would definitely wake up.

Justin was fast asleep with his arse sticking out from under the covers as usual, he was a big bloke and in the state we were in there was no way we were going to pick him up.

"Ok then who's it going to be cos we don't want them to wake up" I said.

A voice from the other side of the room said "Get in bed yer noisy bastards we are trying to sleep" it was Gapper, so that let him off the hook.

Midnight walked over to Suds bed and gave it one hell of a kick, there was a loud bang as the bed bounced off the wall, Suds didn't move.

"He'll do" he said.

So Suds had drawn the short straw, picking up his bed we very slowly moved it to the centre of the room.

"For fucks sake" shouted Gapper "What the fuck are you doing?"

"Shush" says Midnight putting his finger across his lips again, "Give us a hand".

"Not me mate your all fuckin crazy, I don't want anything to do with it, and shut that frickin window it's fuckin freezing in here" he said, lying back down and covering his head with his blankets.

Picking the bed up again we moved towards the open window, lifting it above the sill we got the head end through first then me and Midnight ran outside to the get hold of the other end, which by now was neither in or out of the barrack room but sort of suspended in mid air balancing on the window frame, with the sudden change in air temperature Suds started to stir.

"Oh shit" said Smudge.

We all dived under the bed laughing like demented hyenas.

Suds turned over and then settled down again.

Joined outside by Smudge and Spud we were having trouble lifting the legs at the foot of the bed clear of the sill.

Gapper appeared at the window, grabs the foot end of the bed and gives it one almighty push.

"Now fuck off and let me sleep" he moaned, slamming the window shut.

Suds stirred again and once more we dived for cover but he didn't wake up. This kid could sleep for England.

Picking the bed up again we staggered towards the barrack square, you know, the big tarmac thing that we marched up and down on, looks like a car park, by now we were starting to sober up and realise what we were doing.

"I think we'd better take him back now lads" I said.

While we were debating if we should or not we heard footsteps coming from around the corner.

"Someone's coming" said Spud.

"Quick run" said Smudge.

Then a voice in the distance shouts "Sergeant Parker".

"Oh Christ" I said "It's Nosey Parker".

The footsteps stopped, started again then slowly faded away into the distance.

"Quick let's get to the square before he comes back" said Midnight.

We left poor Suds in bed in the middle of the barrack square and ran back to the barrack room, our intention was to send someone to wake him before morning, but we all fell asleep.

The next morning at 6.30 Nosey Parker came into the room as usual with his hands on cock routine to wake us up.

"Who the fucks missing" he demanded to know, looking at the empty bed space.

Midnight looked at me, I looked at Smudge.

"Ah fuck, Suds" exclaimed Spud, as last night's little escapade suddenly dawned on us.

"And where is ah fuck Suds?" asked Nosey Parker.

But before anyone could answer we heard someone in the distance screaming like a banshee.

"That's the RSM" said Nosey, running out of the room.

Now Regimental Sergeant Major 'Knocker' Knowles was and in all fairness can only be described as a bastard.

We, of course knew what the problem was, he had found Suds, we followed Nosey out towards the barrack square.

There was Suds standing bolt upright to attention on his bed wearing only his underpants, wondering what the fuckin hell had happened to him and how the hell he had got there, the RSM was stomping around the bed kicking it and screaming like a madman, waving his pace stick at Suds demanding an explanation but Suds just stared down at him in disbelief.

Knocker turned and saw Nosey running toward him.

"Is this o'rrable fuckin thing yours Sergeant?" he demanded to know.

"Yes Sir" replied Nosey.

"Take it away, its offensive to my square" screamed Knocker.

The square, as everyone in the army knows, is the pride and joy of every Regimental Sergeant Major in the land and god help those who venture near it that is unless you are on parade which the RSM seemed to be permanently. Every day you could see him with his pace stick open at the correct marching pace, trooping up and down giving himself orders and humming some regimental tune has he went, stopping only to pick up the smallest speck of dirt.

I think the 'mental' in regimental just about sums it up.

Nosey double marched Suds away and we grabbed his bed and returned to the barrack room where they were waiting for us. Not having a lot of choice in the matter we confessed all. Sergeant Parker left it at that for the time being saying he would deal with us later.

Suds on the other hand just did not see the funny side of it and asked to be moved to another section in another room, he got his wish. There were now eight of us, at this rate there will be no one left in our section by the time we finish our training.

Later we heard from Lance Corporal 'Jacko' Jackson that the RSM and 'Nosey' Parker had, had a good laugh about it over a drink in the Sergeants mess. Huh, Knocker Knowles laugh I wish I could have seen that. We didn't actually get away with it, and ended up with extra guard duties, cookhouse fatigues, area cleaning and a whole host of other shit jobs, but that wasn't the last time we had a laugh with an army bed.

Late one night we were awoke by the incessant squeaking of bed springs. It was Taffy bashing his bishop again, that lad just couldn't leave it alone.

On laundry days he had to break his sheets over the end of the bed before he could fold them, they were that stiff.

"Anyone we know?" asked Smudge.

"Two's up" shouts Midnight.

"Give up, you'll wear it out or go blind" I said.

"Haaaaaa!" moaned Taffy.

"Thank fuck for that, now can we get back to sleep" said Spud.

"Alright for you, I've got to sleep with it now" said Taffy.

"Fuck off you dirty bastard, ain't yer got any tissue?" I asked.

"Get yourself a wank sock" said Smudge.

"What the fuck is a wank sock?" asked Taffy.

"A sock you put over yer cock so yer dont cum in yer bed" came the reply.

"He He" chuckled Taffy, "A fuckin wank sock, I never heard of that before".

"But don't use yer army issue one's there as rough as fuck" said Spud.

"Yer you want one of them nice soft civi ones or better still get your lass to send yer a pair of her knickers" said Midnight.

"Preferable unwashed" I said.

"Of course" replied Midnight "There no good if she hasn't had them on".

"You lot get worse", said Justin, who had been laid listening to the conversation.

"Hark who's talking" I remarked to Justin.

"Are you wearing your lasses knickers then Midnight?" I asked.

"Sure am" he says, then he jumps out of bed revealing some white frilly panties with a nice pink bow on the front with his cock sticking out down the side of one leg hole and his balls sticking out down the other, pulling the elasticated leg to one side trying to get his cock back in, he says "Not much room for me bollocks though".

"Hope they look better on your lass then they do on you" laughed Smudge.

"Very nice" I said.

"Sexy" commented Taffy.

"Two's up" said Justin.

"Wouldn't you be better off with my underpants?" asked Spud, throwing a pair of his dirty shreddies at Justin, who caught them had a sniff and threw them back.

"Dirty bastard" he said, "They've got skid marks in them".

"Are you lot going to be quiet now?" asked Schooldays,

"God I'm surrounded by perverts" he said.

We put the lights out and settled back down to sleep.

Smudge got out of bed and was leaving the room.

"Don't forget your sock" said a voice out of the darkness.

"Bollocks" replied Smudge has he left the room.

Every night Company standing orders were posted on the notice board, they were a list of things we needed to know for the next day such as what kit to wear, what was, needed, who was on Commanding Officers orders etc

One night Justin's name was on it.

"Hey Justin you seen standing orders?" I asked

"Not yet" answered Justin.

"Yer names on it you have to see the C. O, what you been up to?" I asked

He went to have a look and on his return he looked puzzled.

"I ain't done nowt wrong, I'm not on a charge or owt" he said.

The next morning we continued with our training and Justin went to his appointment with the C. O.

We meet up with him later that day and asked what he was wanted for.

"Some bastards been spreading stories around that I'm gay" he said.

"Well you are" I said

"And yer did try to fuck Suds with yer soap dildo" said Spud.

"It better not be one of you fuckers" said Justin.

"Anyway what did the C. O. say to you?" I asked.

"There was the C. O, Nosey Parker, and the medical officer, they were asking questions like 'Did I have a girlfriend and did I like girls', 'What did I think of women', they knew all about what happened with Suds and the soap dildo" he explained.

"What did you tell them?" asked Smudge

"Told them it was all an act and that we were just having a bit of fun", then they said 'they were going to keep an eye on me in future and any more reports of this kind would lead to me being chucked out of the army'.

"Who the fuck, reported you then?" I asked.

"Bet it was Suds" said Midnight.

"Look it stands to reason" he continued, "Justin tried to fuck him, we dumped him on the barrack square, then he moved to another section" he explained.

"Yep, you are probably right" I said.

"The grassing little bastard, I'll fuckin kill him" said Justin setting off towards the room that Suds was in.

Midnight grabbed him, "Hold on a minute if you do anything to him now you will really be in the shit" he said.

"OK, then let's put all this stupid army training into practice and do this right" I said.

"What, we going to do, get him outside on his own, when no one's looking?" asked Smudge.

"No" I said continuing "Gather around I will explain".

We all huddled together in a group.

Late that night when everyone was asleep, we sneaked into the room that Suds was in, there were nine other lads in this room and we didn't want to wake any of them.

Without making a sound or speaking to each other we picked up Suds bed and lifted it onto the top of two of steel lockers, he was now balanced about six foot off the ground and fast asleep in his bed. We then retreated into the corridor and set off the fire alarm, all hell broke loose, the noise was incredible, everyone in the whole barrack block woke up, we stayed just long enough to see Suds sit bolt upright, hit his head on the light fitting, swing his legs round as if to get out of bed then fall the six feet to the floor quickly followed by his bed which landed on top of him.

"Got yer, you bastard" whispered Justin.

We then hurried back to our room, a few seconds later Nosey Parker comes storming into the room, any quicker and he would have caught us, before he had chance to say anything, Justin sat up in bed and rubbing his eyes, said,

"What the fucks happening Sergeant?"

"Fire, out of your pits and get outside now" he ordered.

We all lined up outside like good little soldiers, by this time the Fire Brigade had arrived and the place was crawling with firemen.

"Oh! I do love a man in uniform" said Justin.

"Shut it yer daft twat" I said.

One fireman emerged from the building and Nosey Parker went to meet him.

"It's alright sergeant it's a false alarm, there is no fire but we found this under an upturned bed" he said, pointing to another fireman who was carrying Suds over his shoulder.

The second fireman laid Suds on the ground.

"He unconscious" he said, giving Suds a blast of oxygen from his air tank. "He's coming round".

"Got a nasty cut on his forehead, better get him to see your medic" said the first Fireman.

Nosey Parker pointed to me and Justin.

"You two go get a stretcher and take him to the medical centre" he ordered.

We loaded Suds onto the stretcher and off we went bouncing him up and down.

"Ouch me arm, I think it's broken" moaned Suds.

"Nearly there" I said, trying to sound all concerned, really not giving a toss if it hurt or not.

"What happened anyway?" asked Suds.

"You fell out of bed and then your bed jumped on top of you and then you set off the fire alarm" said Justin.

"How the fuck did I do that?" asked Suds.

"Don't know, but you did" I said, trying to keep a straight face.

At the medical centre we were met by the medical officer.

"Casualty from the fire?" he asked.

"There weren't a fire Sir" I said.

"No there weren't a fire" repeated Justin, "He fell out of bed and set off the fire alarm".

"Silly boy" said the doc, "How did you do that?"

"Can't remember" said Suds.

Just then Nosey Parker arrived, no doubt to have a word with Suds about what had happened.

"You two back to the barrack room" he ordered,

Justin started to try and explain to Nosey that Suds had fallen out of bed and set off the fire alarm, and for a few seconds Nosey listened to him.

"Don't be so fuckin daft, fallen out of bed, go on back to the barracks with yer and if I find out it's anything to do with you two, you'll be on a charge" said Nosey.

"Nowt to do with me I were asleep" said Justin.

I grabbed Justin's arm and pulled him towards the door.

"Shut it, daft twat, we've got away with it" I whispered.

Back in the barrack room we told the rest of the lads what we had said to Suds and that we had convinced him that it was the truth, we then, all agreed to keep our mouths shut.

No one ever found out what really happen and no one believed that Suds had done it himself, after a while no one cared.

We heard that Suds had gone off to hospital to get his arm set, he also had three stitches in his forehead, but because of the pot on his arm he was unable to continue training for six weeks, he did get some sick leave, which made us a bit jealous but that didn't really bother us, he had missed six weeks training and was back squaded down to the next up and coming platoon, so he had to repeat the last six weeks training all over again.

That was satisfaction enough for Justin.

Revenge is sweet.

Training was coming to an end, during training we had all been badged up as the Yorkshire Brigade, but we were now rebadged with our respective regimental badges ready to go to our chosen regiments.

Midnight and Justin were going to the Duke of Wellington's Regiment. Smudge and Gapper to the Green Howards, Spud and Schooldays to the Prince of Wales, and Taffy and me to the York and Lancaster's, I don't really know why I picked the Y & L probably because they were my home towns regiment and they were stationed in Cyprus.

There we were all bulled up, badged up shining like new pins, looking the same, but different, if you know what I mean, ready for our pass out parade.

All our friends and relatives were invited and were seated on a makeshift stand at the end of the barrack square.

We lined up behind the band, out of sight, outside our barrack block.

"By the left, quick march" was the command.

As we stepped off the band struck up, I don't know the name of the tune but Midnight who I was next to started to sing.

Have you ever had your bollocks in a rat trap.
In a rat trap. In a rat trap.
Have you ever had your bollocks in a rat trap.
In a rat trap. In a rat trap.

"Silence in the ranks" came a very hushed command from one of the NCO's.

Marching onto the square we all tried to look towards the stand without turning our heads, to see if we could spot our relatives. We were marched around a few times and halted in front of the rostrum where the C.O and another officer were stood.

"Private Brown" the officer called out.

Schooldays snaps to attention and marches towards the rostrum, halts, salutes and stands there riveted to the spot.

"For most up and coming recruit" said the officer, and the C.O hands Schooldays a certificate, he salutes again, about turns and returns to the ranks.

"Well Done Brown, that's one up for five platoon" whispered Nosey Parker, when Schooldays marched past him.

"Private Sidebottom" calls the officer.

"That's another one for five platoon" beams Nosey, sticking his chest out with pride.

"Fuck me, Justin's won" I whispered in surprise.
"Probably first prize for the biggest dildo" whispered Midnight.
Justin had reached the rostrum by now.
"For best recruit" said the officer and the C.O hands Justin a small plaque, he salutes, about turns, but because he was holding the plaque in his left hand or because he was so overwhelmed with the occasion, he forgot how to march, instead of right foot forward, left arm back, he went right foot forward right arm forward.
"Fuck me he's waddling like a fuckin duck" said Nosey.
A ripple of hushed laughter went through the ranks.
"Shut it" someone said.
"And the award for the best platoon goes to Five Platoon, Quebec Company" said the officer.
"We've only gone and fuckin done it, a clean sweep" said Nosey, hardly able to contain himself.
Lieutenant Ponsey comes to attention and marches towards the rostrum, dressed in full ceremonial uniform complete with sword which was scrapping on the ground.
"Wants to get a little wheel on the end of that" commented someone in the ranks.
The C.O handed Poncey a large silver cup.
"We've won the cup. We've won the cup, E.I.N.G.O we've won the cup" chanted Justin in a hushed voice.
"Don't know how the fuck we managed that" I said.
"Right turn, Quick march" came the command.
We stepped off and the band started playing once more.

Have you ever had your bollocks in a rat trap
In a rat trap. In a rat trap.
Have you ever had your bollocks in a rat trap
In a rat trap. In a rat trap.

Sings Midnight once more.

Around and around we marched a few more times and to the applause of our relatives we marched off the square.
Back in the barrack room, getting ready to go home on leave, we said our goodbyes to each other, we promised to keep in touch but we knew that some of us would never meet again.

York & Lancaster's

It was 1967, when I joined the York & Lancaster's, who were stationed at

Episkopi barracks in Cyprus.

My first impressions of the Y & L was that they always seemed to be having a parade, the Queen's Birthday parade, the Remembrance Day parade, the every bloody Saturday parade, the C.O's dogs birthday parade, the Sergeant Majors had a fart today parade, you name it we had a parade for it, what was the point of all this marching up and down, except to fill some sort of sadistic fetish of the RSM's ,did the Queen really care if we were having a parade for her birthday.

The RSM, I can't remember his name, was a bigger bastard than Knocker Knowles at Srensell, he would stand in the centre of the square with us marching around him, then he would point his pace stick at no one in particular and shout

"Give that man extra drill Sergeant".

The Sergeant would just grab the nearest man to him, this twat had me on extra drill on my very first parade, I hadn't been on the bloody island a week and I was in trouble.

The barrack blocks were three story affairs, I was on the top floor, once again in '5' platoon, 'B' company, god was I destined to be '5' platoon for the rest of my days.

These rooms were very large with about twenty men to a room, I won't try to introduce you to everyone there are just too many and I can't recall all their names anyway.

Taffy had ended up in a different company, 'C' company I think, so I didn't see much of him.

Because of the climate we only worked until lunch time, then providing we were not on any other duties, the rest of the day was ours to do as we pleased.

Some of the rules seem to have been relaxed you could call a Corporal by his first or nickname and a Sergeant 'Sarge' as long as no one of higher rank was in hear shot.

My bed was in the corner, I always got the corner bed, the further away from the door the better, which was hard to do in this room as there were four doors to each side of the room, leading out on to a veranda at each side of the building.

Across the room from me, I learned, was a lad called Nobby Clarke, he was a few years older than the rest of us and at one time had been a corporal but got busted back down to private, god knows what for, no one was saying and I don't think anyone had the nerve to ask, he still thought he was a corporal, I suppose it takes a bit of getting used to if your busted back to the ranks. He tried to bully other lads into having his own way and getting them to do things for him, he tried it on with me but I was having none of it, so he tried threatening me.

This apparently was why the corner bed was vacant no one wanted to be near him.

In the early hours of one morning I was awoken by the smell of something burning, in the darkness all I could see was a large red circle that looked to be just above Nobbys bed, I put my bedside light on and saw that his mosquito net was on fire, not blazing but smouldering, I jumped out of bed and grabbed the net tearing it down from where it was secured to the ceiling, folding it over and over again on the floor to put the fire out.

Nobby woke up wanting to know what I was doing.

"You were on fire" I said.

"Fuck off before I thump you" said Nobby.

Some of the other lads in the room were also woken up by the shouting and came to see what was happening. I explained to them about his bed being on fire.

"Fuck him" one of them said.

"And thanks" said one of the others, "We could have all been burned".

The next morning Nobby was in a right mood wanting to know what had happened to his mosquito net.

"It was you, I remember seeing you" said Nobby grabbing the front of my shirt, I shoved him away, he clenched his fist to take a swing at me, just as a lad came up behind him and grabbed him by the arm.

"Touch him and you're on a charge Clarkey" he said.

I later found out he was Corporal 'Davy' Jones.

Davy explained to him what had happened during the night, apparently Nobby had come back from the NAAFI pissed up and had fallen asleep with a lit cigarette in his hand. He seemed to be taken aback by this, turning back to me, "Err, Thanks mate, sorry" he said, after that we became quite good mates, which came in handy later on.

Apparently if you have been promoted once and then get demoted it doesn't take long to get promoted back up again, and Nobby soon got his stripes back, not only that, he was made a regimental policeman (RP), it was just the job for a bully.

There had been some trouble in the 1950's on the island between the Greeks and Turk's, I am not going to get into the politics of it, probably America and the UK sticking their noses in where it's not wanted as usual, anyway this meant that now in the 1960's we were sent up to the village of Troodos to where the RAF had some of those giant golf ball things and our job was to guard them.

Now 6,000 feet up a mountain it tends to get a bit cold and when it snows, it's about 10 to 20 feet deep, we were issued with tropical kit and believe me it was bloody freezing at night, through the day it didn't seem real, all this snow and glorious sunshine, it certainly didn't feel like a Mediterranean island.

Usually the duty lasted for a month and to get up there we would normally travel by truck but coming back down was another matter, there always seemed to be plenty of ways to get there, but very few ways to get down.

If the snow was too deep or the weather too bad and the trucks couldn't get through, then we were taken up by helicopter, which was unable to land because there was nowhere for it to land, so we had to jump out, this also meant that the outgoing guard could not board the helicopter, on more than one occasion we had overlapping guards, too many men and not enough beds, and some had to sleep on the floor.

We were taking over the duty one day and this was the first time I had arrived by helicopter, hovering over the side of what looked to me like a cliff face.

"Jump and move out from under the helicopter as soon as you hit the ground" said the officer in charge.

All the lads just jumped one by one with no problem, landing in the snow they picked up their gear they moved off.

I looked at the officer in the helicopter.

"Go on then" he said "Jump".

"How high are we?" I asked.

"Only about ten feet" he replied.

I jumped, ten foot my fuckin arse it was more like thirty, I landed in the snow and promptly disappeared up to my waist and unable to move I was quickly followed by a dozen pairs of ski's which landed on top of me much to the amusement of the other lads, still laughing they helped me out of the snow, we collected our gear and the ski's together and set off towards the barracks.

"What are the skis's for?" I asked

"To give to the outgoing guard so they can get back down to the snow line and meet the trucks to go back to camp" explained Davy.

"What, they ski down the mountain?" I asked

"That is unless they want to stay here" said another of the lads.

"I hope the snows gone before we go back, I can't fuckin ski" I said.

"Well you've got a month to learn in, or you can stay here" said Davy.

The camp at Troodos was only very small, consisting of a group of huts, there was a permanent staff of a few RAF personal a couple of REME blokes, a couple of blokes from the Royal Signals, a couple of cooks and some Royal Engineers but we didn't have anything much to do with them.

The cookhouse was just a kitchen where you queued up with your tin tray, then went back to your hut to eat your meal. The NAAFI was just a shop where you could buy food, sweets, cigs etc, and that was only open a couple of hours a day, all in all the camp was shit, not a lot to do and nowhere to go, not that you wanted to go outside anyway.

Our barrack room (Hut) had no heating, just a pot bellied stove in the centre of the room, this was fuelled by coke which you had to bring into the hut the night before or you had to dig through the snow the next morning to find it and if you left the shovel outside at night you had to dig through the snow with your bare hands just to get out of the hut. This stove was not that bad once you got it going, great for warming up tins of soup or beans and it made great toast needless to say we never let the fire go out.

To kill the boredom we would play cards, some of us for matchsticks, others for money, we once played Monopoly for real money, pence I might add, not pounds, or should I say 'mils' the Cypriot currency.

Someone had doctored the Monopoly board to read the place names on Cyprus and at one point I was the owner of three hotels in Pathos and four houses on Zig Zag street the notorious red light area of Limasol, I should be so lucky.

I spent quite a bit of time in the Ops room with the lads from the Royal Signals, they were in contact with various military camps around the island, now this was what I wanted to do with my time in the army, I wanted to be a radio operator, so on my return to Episkopi I applied to go on the next available signals cardre.

Our month's duty was soon over and the time had come for us to leave Troodos, I've never been so happy to leave a place in all my life.

Now, did I learn to ski, well I could manage to go in a straight line, at turning I was rubbish, and I wasn't too hot at stopping either, but I need not have worried, the snow had just about gone and the trucks got through.

What is it about a truck load of soldiers that makes them want to sing, you get sat in the back and without any warning someone always bursts into song, you know the sort of thing.

"Four and twenty virgins came down from Inverness and when the ball was over there were four and twenty less singing balls to your partner arse against the wall if you don't get shagged on Saturday night you won't get shagged at all"

Everyone joins in with singing the chorus then each individual has to sing a verse.

"The village Constable he was there the pride of all the force, went they found him in the morning wanking off his horse"

The chorus again, then someone would sing another verse.

The military had their own private beach at Episkopi and nearly every afternoon was spent there, sunbathing, swimming and chatting up the senior NCO's and officers daughters and in some cases their wives.

Of course these girls were ordered by their dads and husbands not to go near the other ranks, but did they take any notice, no way, as they say 'girls will be girls'.

We always wondered if the senior NCO's ordered their wives to have sex by numbers, they did everything else by numbers.

'Panties down, two three, cock in, two three, in out, in out, in out to a regular marching pace'.

I had seen girls in swimsuits before but this was the first time I had ever seen one in a bikini.

Wow! Wobbly bits everywhere.

There was one girl in particular, 'Randy Mandy' the RSM's daughter, now there is a certain pleasure and I don't just mean the sex, in fucking the RSM's daughter, what a way to get back at him.

Now when he gave me extra drill I would think of Mandy and smile to myself, the whole battalion must have been through her in the sand dunes at the back of the beach, we would deliberately kick a beach ball in that direction just to see who was screwing her next.

Evenings on the beach got more livelier once the family men amongst us had gone back home to their married quarters with their wives and little kids, their teenage daughter's on the other hand made all sorts of excuses so they could stay later.

We would build a large bonfire on the beach, some lads would bring guitars and we would sit around talking, and singing the usual dirty songs, there was a game we called the dance of the flaming arseholes, where you each had a certain number of squares of toilet paper which was stuck in a long trail between your bum cheeks and set on fire, then as the flames got closer to your bum you had to war dance around the fire chanting.

'I digga zumbar, zumbar, zumbar
I digga zumbar, zumbar ay
hold em down you Zulu warrior
hold em down you Zulu chief chief, chief'

The one who lasted the longest before running into the sea to extinguish the flames was declared the winner.

One night four UN soldiers arrived at the beach in a white UN Land Rover.

"Fuckin UN, what the fuck do they want" someone said.

As they came walking towards us I was sure I knew at least one of them, it was hard to tell in the dark, all the girls were flocking around them, they were in full uniform immaculately pressed trousers, crisp white shirts, blue berets sporting the white UN cap badge.

Now we as a battalion were not fond of the UN, not because they were allowed to swan about in uniform and we couldn't, who wanted to anyway, it was because they were getting the UN Medal for spending six months on Cyprus and we who were stationed there permanently were not entitled to it.

"Well fuck me drunk" I said as they got closer.

"Its Midnight and Justin" I said

"What the fuck are you doing here?" I asked, greeting them.

"Well for fucks sake", said Midnight "Look who's here".

They explained that some of the Duke's were doing a tour with the UN because the Greeks and Turks were fighting again.

I introduced them to the lads and they joined us around the fire, Midnight and Justin were still surrounded by the girls. Randy Mandy was linking Justin's arm.

"He's no good to you Mandy" I said.

"Why?" she asked, looking up into Justin's eyes.

"He bats for the other team", I said, she didn't quite know what I meant, so I left it at that.

"You speak for yourself" said Justin in his best camp voice.

Before the night was over she had, had both Justin and Midnight in the sand dunes, plus the other two UN lads that came with them.

Now, I was confused, was Justin gay or not, perhaps he bats for both teams.

I must admit it was great to see them again and I told them I was joining the Dukes next year, as the Y&L were being disbanded and I was going to transfer to them.

They told me to put in for the signal platoon, which was a coincidence, because I had just qualified as a radio operator and was a company operator waiting to go into our own signal platoon.

The evening came to an end and we said goodbye to Midnight, Justin and the other two lads, some of the lads were arguing, who's turn it was to take Randy Mandy home and get the last shag of the night, Mandy herself was in between them kissing one, and then the other, she didn't really care which one took her home, in fact she would have been happy if they both did.

That wasn't our main problem, we had to get back into camp and the only way to do that was to go past the guardroom, now the tried and tested method was to act as sober as possible and march passed, there was another way into the camp without passing the guardroom but that meant climbing the 100 foot cliff face that overlooked the beach, I had on occasion climbed down it, but that was in daylight and before I'd had a drink, so there no way we were going to climb up it in the dark while we were pissed, so with no other alternative we headed towards the guardroom, and as always one or more of the duty RP's would be waiting for us.

"Show your I.D. Cards" one would demand.

"Line up, stand to attention" demanded another.

We knew we could end up with all kinds of punishment if we didn't obey, these lads were bastards and knew it.

I was just about to get put through the mill by one of them, when Nobby Clarke came out of the guardroom he looked along the line and saw me.

"Sargeant come here" he said.

I jumped to attention and marched towards him, stamped my foot in, which bloody hurt; I was only wearing flip flops and halted in front of him as steady as a rock. 'What the fuck had I done? What the fuck was he picking on me for?' I thought to myself.

I suppose the answer to that is, because he can.

He leaned forward and pretended to smell my breath.

"You drunk lad?" he asked and without waiting for a reply said "On yer way, and double march up that road".

He didn't have to tell me twice, I was off towards the barrack block like shit off a shovel. I didn't dare look back, but heard the RP's barking orders at the others, and then it dawned on me, the fire, he hadn't forgotten.

On arrival back in England in 1968, we were stationed at an old RAF base at North Weald Epping Essex, we knew by now that the Y & L were being disbanded and had very little to do, the most exciting thing that happen was the filming of The Battle Of Britain film which was taking place at the other end of the airfield, some of the lads were roped in as unpaid extras, otherwise the rest of us were told to stay out of the way.

Nights out at North Weald were a disaster, because of the complaints from the locals, so in the end we were confined to barracks, it seems the locals didn't want us near their daughters but when one of their kids went missing in Epping forest, it was us silly buggers that got called out to search for them.

Thankfully we were not there very long and as the time for the disbandment drew closer we were sent up to Strensell at York, I hadn't been back there since basic training, it hadn't changed a bit.

Our barracks were the old Nissen huts at the far end of the camp, these hadn't been lived in for donkeys years, they were absolutely filthy and were darn near impossible to get clean enough to live in, the more we tried the worse it got, seemed like we were just moving muck from one place to another, then someone had the bright idea to turn the fire hose on and drown the place, so we stripped down to just our shorts and let rip with the hose, it works the muck was gone in seconds, but it took hours for the rooms to dry out, no problem, let's go to the NAAFI.

We virtually took over the NAAFI, on the understanding that we kept out of the way of the lads who were doing their training and it seemed the camp staff just left us alone, I don't think we would have taken any notice of them anyway. The trainee's had to march has they walked from place to place on the camp, we on the other hand would just saunter along and please our self's, on a couple of occasions some of our lads got pulled up by the odd Sarn't Major or officer but as soon as they saw we were Y & L they just sent us on our way.

On being disbanded we marched through the city of Sheffield and some other Yorkshire towns that the regiment was affiliated to, we laid our colours up in

Sheffield Cathedral, where we had a service, and the Y & L's left the ranks of the British army forever, you would have thought someone had died, well I suppose in a way they had, I have never seen so many rough tough raggy arsed soldiers with tears in their eyes in all my life.

Duke of Wellington's

The Duke of Wellington's Regiment, affectionately known by us as: The Sheep Shaggers.

The landing at Hong Kong airport in the 1960's was the scariest I have ever seen, the plane comes down to below the level of the tops of the skyscrapers and fly's in between them, you can see right into people's homes, some even waved at you as you went passed.

We were picked up from the airport by truck and driven to Stanley Fort Barracks, on the way the usual thing happened.

Dina, Dina, show us your leg, show us your leg, show us your leg
Dina, Dina, show us your leg, a yard above your knee

A rich girl wears a brassier a poor girl uses string
But Dina users nothing at all she lets the fucker's swing

Soldiers and trucks again.

On arrival at Stanley Fort the truck pulled up outside a barrack block, where we were ordered to line up, our names were called out and we were directed to our respective companies, most of the lads seemed to be going into rifle company's, I stood there praying, 'please let me be in the signal platoon', I had applied but I was not sure if I had been successful, by now a group of the Duke's had congregated on the balcony of the barrack block and were looking down at us, I could see Justin and Midnight amongst them.

"Private Sargeant signals platoon" called the NCO.

A loud cheer went up from the balcony, and I punched the air with my fist, just what I wanted.

"They expecting you?" asked the NCO.

"Looks like it" I replied.

"Well go on then get up there" he said.

"Get up here" shouted Justin.

I grabbed my kit and couldn't get up those stairs fast enough. I was met halfway up by two other lads.

"Hi, I'm Frank, give us your cases" he said.

"Hi, and I'm Rod" said the other.

On the top floor we met Justin, who grabbed me and gave me a hug.
"Get off me yer daft bugger" I told him.
"We've heard all about you" said Frank.
'Oh! Christ, what had Justin been saying' I thought.
"Justin said you were coming into our platoon", said Frank.
"How did he know?" I asked.
"Put in a good word for you with our CO, I told him you were a wizz kid with radios and stuff" said Justin.
"In fact we were that sure we were getting you that we got your bed ready, so you don't have to go to the stores" said Frank, pointing towards the corner of the room.
'The corner bed again', I thought, 'How do I do it'.
I unpacked my kit and settled in, I was made really welcome it felt like I had been with these lads all the time and not just met them.
"What do you do for entertainment?" I asked.
"Nothing tonight, probably just go to the NAAFI for a few San Migs, we're waiting for pay day, then it's off down town to Wan Chai", said Rod.
"What's San Mig?" I asked.
"The local beer, there is also Tiger beer, but that's like battery acid" said someone else.
"And before you ask, Wan Chai is the town where we go drinking, down Lockhart Road, there's a bar, a brothel, a tattooist, a bar, a brothel, a tattooist, all the way along it" said Rod.
"Or we could meet the girls" said Frank.
"Which girls are these?" I asked.
"You'll see, all in good time" replied Frank.

The next morning we were lined up outside the barrack block on parade and morning inspection, we would normally be inspected and given our respective jobs for the day by our platoon Sgt, but this morning it was our platoon commander Captain Red, well that's what we called him. He walked along the line of men and stopped when he got to me.
"You must be Private Sargeant?" he asked.
"Yes Sir" I replied.
"You came with glowing references" he said, turning towards Justin and continuing, "Didn't he Sidebottom?"
"Yes Sir" answered Justin.
"Right Sarn't, I'm off" he said, turning to our platoon Sgt, who saluted him, he returned the salute and left.
"Private Sargeant report to the lecture rooms after parade" he said.
He then gave the rest of the lads their jobs and dismissed the parade.
"Where is the lecture room and what do I have to report there for?" I asked Justin.

"To watch the blobby nob film" he replied.

"Watch the what?" I asked.

"The blobby nob film, we all had to watch it, it's about VD, they show you pictures of blobby nobs, tell you about the prostitutes and give you some condoms, but you'll not need them" said Justin.

"Why won't I need them?" I asked.

"All in good time", answered Justin.

'That's twice I've been told that' I thought.

I went to watch the blobby nob film, and collected a nice big handful of condoms, well you never know they might come in handy, but the film was enough to put you off sex for life.

Later that day I was told by the platoon sergeant that I was to go on a grade 3 signals cardre starting new week.

"Hang on a minute sarge, I'm already a grade 2" I said.

"I got my grade 2 with the Y & L's" I continued.

"We need to know, what you know" he explained.

"Yer, but it's not fair making me do the grade 3 again, is it" I protested.

"It's either that or back to a rifle company" he said.

Eventually we came to a compromise and I sat through the grade 3 cardre again, but passed the extended grade 3 exams at the end, therefore keeping my grade 2 statuses. In fact the only difference between the grades is that one has a faster Morse code speed than the other.

I was now more qualified than most of our NCO's, which then caused another problem, because in order to be an NCO in the signals platoon you had to have the

grade 1 qualification, so all our NCO's sat the grade 1 exam, and of course they all passed, now normally the grade 1 is instructed by the Royal Signals, which still begs the question, who taught them and who took them for the exam, there wasn't anyone qualified in the signal platoon to do that, with hindsight, I think I know what the problem was, some of the ex Y & L's that had gone to the rifle company's, were not getting on with the Duke's ,there was a lot of animosity between them, unlike myself who had settled in straight away, perhaps this was because of the fact that I already knew Justin and Midnight, that may have helped me settle in.

The others were staying within their own little groups and not mixing, this meant that they were being passed over for promotion and other cushy numbers (good easy jobs), and they didn't like it. It seemed that there was no way the Duke's were ever going to promote an ex Y & L.

I personally couldn't have cared less, I was quite happy doing what I was doing and being a private.

Life in the barracks was great, we had a boot boy (Mick) who cleaned and bulled everyone's boots and shoes for $5 (dollars) a week each, how he knew who's were who's boots I never knew, we just left them on the floor and by the next morning they were under your bed, cleaned and ready to wear. He would come around every pay day to collect his money and as always some of the lads tried to avoid him, you could hear him running around the barrack block chasing the ones who hadn't paid, shouting

"You owe me five dolla", in his best English voice, we all paid up eventually because he would go to the company commander and complain.

When pay day finally came around, that was it we were off for a night on the town, look out Wan Chai we're on our way. The night out always started with a visit to the 'Iron Duke' a bar named after the Duke of Wellington in the village of Stanley just down the road from the camp, the name of this bar changed with each incoming regiment, it was only a small place with about a dozen tables and was always packed out, standing room only, a few San Migs and then a taxi to Wan Chai, where the night out really started with a visit to the China Fleet Club which was owned and run by the Navy, it was really for the sailors who were in port, and was like a giant NAAFI but with a cinema and accommodation, so if you were too pissed to get back to camp, you just booked in here.

A mixed grill, and a few more bottles of San Mig, and we were ready to hit the bars.

The lad's favourite bar was The Mermaid Bar on Lockhart Road, this was my first trip to one of these bars so I just tagged along behind.

"Hey Flankie you come back, see us" said a rather large women as we entered the batwing doors.

"Hey Mamma San" said Frank, throwing his arms around her.

She greeted each one of the lads in turn by either their name of nickname, how on earth did she remember everyone, bring up the rear, she grab me and nearly squeezed the living daylights out of me.

"Hey Flankie, you bring me nice new boy" and without waiting for a reply from Frank she turned back to me.

"What your name handsome?"

"Sarge" I said.

"Sarge, you no Sarge, you nice boy, you come sitty down I find you nice girl" she said.

The bar was virtually in darkness apart from the lights behind and around the bar, in front of the bar was a row of stools and up each side there were booths that seated four people.

The Mamma San lead us to a booth and we ordered four beers, when the beers arrived so did one of the bar girls, she was a small petite looking thing wearing the shortest skirt and the lowest top you have ever seen, shoving herself between me and the table she sat on my lap.

"You buy me drink?" she asked.

"Ok" I said.

She clicked her fingers and another girl brought her a drink in shot class, which she downed in one go.

"Ten dolla" said the girl who had brought the drink.

"What ten fuckin dollars" I said.

The girl had already drunk the drink so having no choice I paid.

"You buy me more drink?" asked the girl.

"On yer bike Susie Wong" I said pushing the girl off my lap.

The other lads by now were laughing their cocks off.

"You could have warned me" I said.

"Why, we thought you were doing ok" said Justin.

"What was she drinking anyway?" I asked.

"Cold tea" replied Frank.

"At ten dollars a chuck, you lousy bastards", I said.

"It's best not to have anything to do with the bar girls, they don't fuck and you can't touch" explained Frank.

"Right just for that, get the beers in it's your round" I said

After a few more beers we moved onto another bar called

The Kings Bar, on the way there we were stopped every few yards by pimps.

"You want pussy?" asked one of the pimps.

"No thanks love" said Justin, in a camp voice "I don't like cats".

"You want boy me find you good boy" said the Pimp.

"How much?" asked Justin.

"You follow me we find good boy twenty dolla, him plenty suck suck" said the Pimp.

"Too much, I only got ten dollars" replied Justin.

"Too cheap, you plenty money for good boy" said the Pimp.

Justin by now was tiring of this and started walking away when Frank turned to the pimp and asked,

"You got young girl, how much for sixteen year old virgin?"

"Plenty virgin fifty dolla" replied the Pimp.

"She'll be about fifty years old he means and everyone in Wan Chai will have been through her" said Rod.

We set off walking away and the pimp followed us, still trying to get us to go with him, but he must have strayed out of his area because another pimp blocked his way and stated to argue with him.

"Why not go with him?" I asked, "I could do with a fuck".

"We don't go with the prostitutes, you don't know how clean they are and we don't want a dose of clap" explained Rod.

"Besides, some of the brothels are out of bounds and if you get caught in them you're on a charge" said Frank.

"Yep, two lads from 'C' company got fourteen days on Stonecutters last week, for it" said Rod.

"What's Stonecutters?" I asked.

"Stonecutters Island, it's the military prison, and believe me you don't want to go there", explained Rod.

"Why, have you been?" I asked.

"No but the lads who have say its murder, the MP's give you some right shit" said Rod.

"I could still do with a fuck though" I said.

"We'll be seeing the girls soon, wait until then" said Justin.

"If you can't wait then have a wank" said Rod.

"Or ask Justin to give you one" said Frank, laughing.

"Yer right" commented Justin "Like fuck I will".

"Are you right handed Sarge?" asked Rod.

"Yep" I answered.

"Then try wanking with your left hand, it feels like someone else is doing it for you" replied Rod.

"Left handed wank" commented Frank, "Is that what you do Rod?" he asked.

"Yer but I am left handed" replied Rod.

"Well in your case try a right handed wank" said Frank.

"Anyway, who are these girls we're seeing soon?" I asked.

"All in good time" answered Justin.

"That's the third time you've told me that, what's the big secret?" I asked.

"You'll see" answered Justin.

The Kings bar was no different to the Mermaid, the same lay out just different people, we walked in and found the place was packed out, managing to get to the bar we order drinks but had to stand there drinking them.

"You new boy?" asked the barman.

"No" I replied.

"I never seen you before" he said, turning to the tall thin woman seated at the end of the bar, he spoke to her in Chinese.

"Look out" said Frank.

"What's wrong?" I asked.

But before Frank could reply the tall thin woman came and put her arm around me.

"Hello sailor you like Mamma San, me find you nice girl" she said.

"No thanks" I said, thinking 'once bitten twice shy'.

"You lovely boy, you want nice girl" she continued.

"No thanks" I said again.

Seeing I was getting annoyed, Justin whispered something to the woman and she immediately stopped pestering me and walked away.

"What did you say?" I asked.

"Oh! Nothing" was his reply.

"Well whatever it was it worked, thanks" I said.

"He told her you were gay" said Frank.

"What! Well at least it got rid of her" I said, and with that I kissed Justin on the cheek.

"Get off, what the fuck you doing?" asked Justin.

"That'll teach yer to tell them I'm gay" I replied, grabbing him, we skipped out of the bar hand in hand, much to the amusement of the other lads.

By the early hours of the morning, we were feeling worse for wear, the drinking was taking its toll, so it was decided the best thing to do would be to head back to the barracks.

Rod jumped in a rickshaw, the driver or puller, which ever you want to call him, picked up the handle.

"Where we go?" he asked.

"Stanley Fort" demanded Rod

The driver dropped the handle to the floor and Rod went arse over tit onto the road.

"I no go Stanley Fort, too far, I no go, you bugger off" resorted the driver.

"I knew he would do that" said Rod, picking himself up off the ground and laughing his silly head off.

"Happens every time, he gets pissed and tries to get a rickshaw" commented Frank, has he flagged down a taxi.

On the way back to Stanley, Justin was in the front seat, I was sat in the middle in the back with Rod and Frank, about half way there Rod wanted to stop because he was feeling sick.

"You no be sicky in my car" shouted the driver, and promptly stopped at the side of the road.

Rod jumped out, tried to play the yellow trombone and made other various noises, but he couldn't be sick so he got back into the taxi and we set off again, still a few miles from camp he said he wanted to be sick again.

"Wind the window down" said Frank.

Rod fumbles for the handle, finds it and winds it down.

"Shut the fuckin window it freezing" demanded Justin.

So Rod shut the window, but a bit farther on, he wants to be sick again and reopens it.

"For fuck sake Rod, shut the bleedin window" demanded Justin again.

So Rod shut the window again and seemed to settle down.

"Thank fuck for that, moaned Justin.

Just then Rod sat up, trying to open the window again.

"I'm going to be sssssssssiiiiiiicccccc....." he tried to say, too late he wasn't quick enough and threw up all over the inside of the car, the driver got it down the back of his neck, Justin had his head turned towards Rod and got a face full, now call me a coward if you like, but I was in the middle sat next to Rod, I pulled Frank over towards Rod and hid behind him trying to avoid the stream of projectile vomit that was about to head my way.

It wasn't a taxi anymore, we were a disaster area, if we had been a third world country the government would have declared a state of emergency.

The driver stopped, jumped out of the car ranting, raving and screaming his bloody head off.

"You basta, you basta, you sicky in my car, you clean, me report to guard, you clean, you pay me" he ranted.

We pulled Rod out of the car, by now he was fast asleep and couldn't give a fuck what was happening, there was nothing to clean the car with so we took off our shirts and used them, then threw them away into the bushes, I wouldn't have minded but I had only just bought that shirt to go out in that night, we cleaned up best we could but were unable to do anything about the smell, the driver was still ranting and raving, you couldn't blame the bloke, he had a living to earn and Rod had fucked it up good and proper, but we were getting a bit sick (excuse the pun) of listening to him.

"Shut the fuck up" Justin said to him.

"You fuckey up, you fuckey up, me want money, me want money" he demanded.

We chucked Rod back into the car with the intentions of continuing our journey, but the driver dragged him back out again.

"I no take you, you pay me and I go" he said.

Normally the journey from Wan Chai to Stanley cost about $10, Justin felt in Rod's trouser pocket and pull out a sick laden $50 note, throwing it at the diver he told him to fuck off.

Left with the unconscious Rod at the side of the road, still about four miles from camp.

"What the fuck we going do now" I asked.

"Fuck knows" said Frank.

"We could leave the silly bastard here to rot" said Justin.

"It's a still a long way back to camp" said Frank.

"Suppose we'll have to carry the silly git" said Justin, looking down at Rod who was still on the ground.

"That's not the main problem, we have to get passed the guardroom with him" I said.

Usually if you were in a taxi, the RP's would just wave you through, but if you were walking and one or more of you were drunk then you were in the shit.

Rod was out of it completely so what were we going to do, it was now about 5am, we had been walking and carrying Rod for about half an hour and were absolutely shattered.

"Listen, there's something coming up the hill" said Frank.

We stopped to listen and around the corner came one of our Land Rovers.

"The mail run" said Frank.

"Thank fuck for that" said Justin jumping into the middle of the road to flag it down.

"Want a lift boy's?" asked Captain Red.

"Please Sir" said Justin, as we slung Rod into the mail sacks in the back.

"I won't ask you what you're doing" said Red.

And not one of us offered him an explanation.

Having an officer in the front of the Land Rover made it easy to get passed the guardroom, the RP just saluted us as we drove straight through. Red dropped us off outside our barrack block we dragged Rod up the steps and dumped him on his bed.

The bars in Hong Kong stayed open while ever there was someone in them, most just shut for an hour in the morning to sweep up and throw the drunks out, then reopened again.

The drinks were cheap at around a dollar a bottle, at that time one Hong Kong dollar was about one shilling and four pennies in old money or about nine pence in today's money, that was until an American ship came in, either on its way to or from Vietnam loaded up with soldiers and sailors on R & R, then the beer went up to $5 a bottle, usually we didn't bother going down town if they were in port, the lads said it was too expensive for them.

On the odd occasion we did go, it was to find an American who was that pissed that if you sat and listened to his Vietnam war stories all night, he would buy the beer.

They were not hard to find, they were always in full uniform, we were not allow to wear ours off camp, but like I've said before 'who wants to'.

Sat in the Mermaid Bar one night, the Mamma San only charged us the normal price of $1 a bottle, but we weren't to let on to the Americans.

Me and Frank were talking to two rather drunk American sailors one night, each had a bar girl sat on their laps, when Frank asked what all the medal ribbons on their uniforms were for.

"That's the Nam medal" said one, in a southern drawl.

"We all got that one" then pointing to each ribbon in turn he continued along the row.

I can't remember exactly how the description of his medals went, but it was something like this.

"That's the sharp shooter medal, that's the best turned out sailor medal, that's the top in my section medal" said the Sailor has he gave a detailed description of each ribbon, all of which seemed to be bloody pointless to us.

"Don't yer get medals for bravery and stuff?" asked Frank.

"Yep, sure do, show the dude the Purple Heart Buck" he said, turning to the sailor next to him.

Buck pointed to a ribbon on his chest.

Frank put his finger out to touch the ribbon and said,

"Wow! so that's a purple heart".

"You got wounded in Nam then?" he asked.

"Well me and Billy Bob was riding in the back of a truck in Nam when I fell out and broke my darn leg and ...."

Frank cut him short in mid sentence, pointing back at the ribbons, he said,

"That's for sweeping up, that's for wiping my arse, that's for chewing my gum, that's a gravy stain, that's for being a pillock", then pointing back to the purple heart again, said "That's for falling off a truck".

Frank then opened out his arms, shrugged his shoulders, looked directly at the sailors, and said, "And, that's what you get when you allow cousins to marry".

"Fer fucks sake Frank, shut it" I said.

"Fuck them, the big headed twats" he replied.

But I needn't have worried, they were too far pissed to care or maybe it was probably because they were having trouble understanding Frank's thick Yorkshire accent, either way they didn't seem to realise that they had just been insulted.

While all this was going on the sailors kept on ordering more drinks, two for themselves, two for Frank and myself and two for the bar girls, with the inflated prices because they were in port, it was costing them $60 dollars a round for just six drinks, the bar was ripping them off something rotten, but what the hell did we care, they were the one's who were paying not us, more money than brains these guys. Well not just these two the bar was packed with Americans, some of which hadn't got any Hong Kong money and were paying in American dollars, so if they were buying the same drinks as the guys we were with, then it was costing them the equivalent of about $240 Hong Kong dollars a round.

We once tried to explain it to them, but they just didn't understand.

At the end of the night Buck and Billy Bob were really drunk so we helped them back to their ship, the journey was within walking distance of Lockhart Road, but they were staggering all over the place and we didn't want them to get picked up by our MP's or their Shore Patrol, so we took Rickshaws, normally a Rickshaw ride costs just one dollar, but as soon as the driver saw the sailors the price shot up to $10.

Their ship was the USS Penobscot, not a very big vessel by American standards, but big enough I suppose.

Buck and Billy Bob invited us on board to have a look around, the guard at the end of the gangway didn't seem to care who we were and didn't ask for any ID or even try to stop us from boarding, try to walk onto a British navy ship and see what happens.

USS Penobscot as I said was not a large ship but once inside it was like a floating five star hotel, talk about home comforts, if I lived on here I wouldn't want to go home, they do live a rough life these Americans, it had Coca Cola machines, chocolate bar machines, chewing gum machines, machines you could get snacks from, a pool tables, one armed bandits, TV's and the galley (kitchen) was open serving food all day and night. I had been on British ships, and they were cramped by comparison, even our big ships were cramped compared to their small ones and the meals on our ships were on small tin tray three times a day that always left you feeling hungry, that may have been OK for our sailors who didn't have a lot of room to move about in and therefore probably didn't need as much food, but we were soldiers and ate two tatter's more than a pig, as for the other stuff, well forget it, you were lucky if you had a pack of cards and a dart board, no darts, just the board.

Justin walked into the barrack room.

"Just been on the phone to Tammy, we're meeting them on Stanley beach at one" he said.

"Will Lily and Monica be there?" asked Frank.

"Yep, their all coming and their bringing Jeanie for Sarge" replied Justin.

"What's Jeanie like?" I asked

"About five foot four small tits nice bum" answered Rod.

"Trust you to notice her tits and bum" said Justin.

"What else is there?" asked Rod.

"What about their minds, their intellect, their feelings" said Frank.

"Sod their minds, I don't want to fuck her mind and the only thing Monica will be feeling is this" said Rod, holding his crotch and thrusting his hips forward.

"So who are they? Bar girls" I asked answering my own question.

"Go on tell him Justin, you've kept him in suspense long enough" said Frank.

"They call themselves college girls and their all about twenty years old training to be lawyers, accountants and other top jobs like that, they live in Shaukiwan near the college" said Justin.

"How did you lot meet them?" I asked.

"We were out shopping and Tammy was working part time in one of the shops, Justin took a fancy to her and chattered her up", she then introduced Lily and Monica to me and Rod, and we've been going out ever since" said Frank.

"Before we meet them, don't tell them you have been with a bar girl or a prostitute or Jeanie won't have anything to do with you" said Justin.

"I haven't" I said.

"We tried to get her off with one of the other lads but she wouldn't have anything to do with him" said Frank.

"We didn't know why at first then Tammy told Justin what Jeanie had said to her about prostitutes" said Rod.

"Well I don't blame her" I said.

"Same applies to us, if we go with the bar girls and pro's, that's why we don't bother with them when we go down town" said Frank.

"So I can take it as read, that you lot are shagging the arses off these girls then?" I said.

"Correct" answered Rod.

"What chance have I got with Jeanie then?" I asked.

"Wait and see it's up to her" said Frank.

"Better take some condoms with me then" I said.

"You'll not need them" said Justin.

"Why? I might have the chance of a fuck, or does she ride bareback?" I asked.

"No way, they all use condoms" said Frank.

"So why don't I need them?" I asked again.

"Because they bring their own, they don't like army issue and complain that there too thick, when we meet them on the beach, they usually strip off into their bikini's, if they do look at their bums and if you can see the outline of the ring of a condom in its packet on the inside of their bikini bottoms you're in with the chance" explained Frank.

"I'll probably not be able to keep my eyes off their bums or any other bits for that matter" I said.

"Randy bastard calm down" said Justin.

We arrived at Stanley beach just before 1pm, in time to meet the bus from Shaukiwan, I went with Rod to get some beers, by the time we got back Frank and Justin had met the girls and they were walking along the beach.

"Hey! Wait for us" shouted Rod.

They stood and waited, as we caught them up, they started walking again.

"Hello" said one of the girls to me,

"Hi" I replied.

"Hi, I'm Tammy, this is Lily, this is Monica and this is Jeanie" she said, introducing the girls.

Tammy was linking Jason's arm, Lily with Frank and Monica was doing the same with Rod, by now I was feeling a bit apprehensive, then Jeanie moved closer to me, caught hold of my hand and we walking up the beach holding hands.

They were all very good looking girls, not one of them was wearing a scrap of makeup, they didn't need it they were beautiful.

The girls as predicted stripped off into their bikinis, except Tammy who was still wearing her shorts and shirt, for some reason she didn't strip off all day, was Jeanie carrying a condom or not, I looked at the other girls.

Yes, lily was, and Monica looked to have two in her bikini bottoms, it looked like Rod was in for a good night, or was she just carrying a spare. Jeanie stripped off to reveal a skimpy pale blue bikini she turned her back towards me,

'What a fantastic little body' I thought has she stood up straight and ran her fingers around the inside edge of the elastic leg of her bottoms, I couldn't see the outline of a condom anywhere, never mind this was the first time we'd met and we didn't really know each other, so I couldn't expect miracles.

We played a few games of volley ball, now there's a sight to behold, girls in bikini's playing volley ball, believe me it wasn't just the ball that was bouncing.

The lads and their respective partners were sat on the beach kissing and cuddling, Jeanie took my hand and we walked towards the children's play area, where

I sat on one of the swings, thinking that Jeanie would sit on the next swing I was a bit surprised when she lifted one leg up and put it between the swing rope and me then did the same with the other leg to sit on my lap facing me. I was now sat in between her legs, I gave the swing a gentle push backwards with my feet and she shuffled forward closer to me, to stop her sliding backwards away from me I placed my hands on her bum and she put her arms around my neck, she hadn't spoken very much all day.

"Hello you" she said looking up into my eyes.

"Hello you" I replied.

"How old are you?" she asked.

"I'm twenty" I replied, "How old are you?"

"Same, twenty" she said.

"Do you go to Wan Chai?" she asked.

I was ready for this question, "Sometimes", I replied.

"You, not been with bar girl?" she asked.

"No I haven't, I don't like them" I said, trying to think of a better answer.

"Good" she said, shuffling a little closer.

By now there was hardly any fresh air between us; it was only her bikini bottoms and my shorts that were actually stopping us from having sex.

We must have sat like this for hours, she very rarely spoke again, except to ask me if I want to kiss her, what was wrong with me, I hadn't even thought about kissing her.

She lifted her head up and I kissed her, at the same time I squeezed her bum.

Oh! Christ what is happening to me.

I was happy, very happy in fact just to sit there holding her, and I must admit I had a huge erection and I suspected she knew I had too, there was no way she could not have known, she was just about sat on it.

Every time the swing slowed down I pushed it a little harder and every time I did, she edged even more closer and the closer she got, the more she was rubbing on my erection, then she let out a little moan and I felt all her body shudder has she squeezed me tighter with her legs. I realised she'd had an orgasm. She then realised that I knew that she had.

"Sorry" she whispered, without lifting her head from my shoulder.

"It's OK" I whispered, to her.

Then she had another orgasm, then another.

"Please stop pushing the swing" she said, "You're driving me crazy".

I stopped the swing and we just sat there laughing at each other.

"You make me cum and we not even do jig a jig" she said, still laughing.

"What are you two laughing at?" asked Tammy, who was walking towards us with Justin.

"Oh! Nothing" I replied.

Then Jeanie said something in Chinese and Tammy burst out laughing, and walked away with Justin, I heard them both laughing as they went, so I assume that Jeanie had told Tammy what had just happened on the swing and then Tammy had told Justin.

"What about you?" asked Jeanie, casting her eyes downward at my erection?

"Don't worry" I said.

"Jeanie" shouted Monica, "Tammy says this is for you" she said, handing Jeanie the spare condom.

"We go jig a jig now, if you want" she said.

'If I want' I thought, 'Of course I want'.

"Only if you want to" I said, hoping that she wouldn't change her mind.

"Come with me" she said.

I stood up.

"I can't go like this" I said, pointing at my erection which was sticking out in front under my shorts. Jeanie shouted something in Chinese to Tammy and she picked up my shirt and threw it to her, I held it in front of me while we walked hand in hand to the far end of the beach.

I laid my shirt on the sand and we both sat down, Jeanie pushed me onto my back and sat straddled across me, rubbing herself against me she moaned again and squeezed me with her thighs, she leaned forward and we kissed, then lifted herself off me and unfastened my shorts, ripping the condom from its packet she placed it on my erection then removing her bikini bottoms she straddled me again and allowed me to slip inside her.

With our arms around each other we walked slowly back along the beach. It was starting to get dark by now.

"We know what you've been doing" said Frank.

"Shut up" said Jeanie, blushing.

Jeanie sat with the other girls who were chatting away in Chinese to each other.

I sat with the lads and had a few beers, they wanted to know what it was like with Jeanie, I refused to tell them anything, after a while Jeanie came back to me and we lay on the sand kissing and cuddling.

Justin and Tammy walked off up the beach one way and Lily and Frank walked off in the other direction, we knew they were going to find a quite spot so they could have sex.

Rod and Monica stayed with us.

'Why weren't they going' I wondered.

I was getting aroused again laid there with Jeanie, she was all over me, one minute she was on top of me the next I was rolling on top of her.

"Will you two pack it in, haven't you had enough" said Rod.

"You want more jig a jig?" asked Jeanie, whispering in my ear.

"I don't have a condom" I said.

Jeanie turned to Monica, spoke again in Chinese, and Monica threw her the other condom.

"Come" she said, pulling me up off the sand.

The evening came to an end, and we walked the girls back to the bus stop, when the bus arrived Jeanie kissed me, gave me a piece of paper with her phone number on and told me to ring her tomorrow. They boarded the bus and we all waved goodbye as it pulled away.

"You jammy bastard" said Frank.

"Two shags and poor old Rod gets nowt" said Justin.

"He only got two shags because Monica gave Jeanie her condom" complained Rod.

"Don't you ever talk to that girl?" asked Justin looking at Rod.

"No, I wanna fuck her to death not talk her to death" said Rod.

"If you had taken the time to talk to her, you would have known that she likes to be in control when she has sex, not like you wham bam thank you ma'am" explained Justin.

"How do you know?" asked Rod.

"Tammy told me" answered Justin.

"If you keep treating her like shit, she will dump you" said Frank.

Rod just sort of grunted, as if to show his disapproval.

"You seeing Jeanie again?" asked Frank.

"Yep, I got her phone number" I replied.

"It must be love" commented Justin.

"Come on then Sarge tell us what she's like, is she a good shag?" asked Rod.

"Mind your own business, and anyway a gentlemen never tells" I said.

"Gentleman, get you, you big strong thing" said Justin.

"Anyway no man's gentle, ask Rod's sister" said Frank.

"Have you been with Rod's sister then?" I asked him.

"No, but to hear Rod talk about her, she's been with everyone else" answered Frank.

"Shut it about my sister" said Rod.

"Don't blame us you told us about her" said Frank.

"When?" asked Rod.

"When you were pissed a few weeks ago" said Frank.

"I never said anything about my sister" said Rod.

"Yep you did" commented Justin.

"What she can't do with a Mars bar isn't worth talking about" said Frank.

"Shut it, daft twats" said Rod, walking off towards our bus stop.

We caught the bus back into camp, Justin and Frank were still weighing up the pro's and con's of Rod's sister and I was contemplating if I would ever eat another Mars Bar again, the thought of what she was doing with it made me shudder, I don't think I will ever look at one in the same light again.At least while they were ribbing Rod about his sister they were not asking me questions about Jeanie.

I went to read company standing orders and found out I had been allocated the job of looking after the radio room.

'Great' I thought, 'This is the cushy number I've been looking for'. I knew I had to man the radio at least once a day and enter any messages into the log book but I always timed the call for 8am which got me out of attending the morning parade. I had to keep the place clean; otherwise it was a doddle of a job. I collected the keys and went to investigate, any problems and it was my responsibility I was the one in sole possession of the keys.

The radio room was on top of what looked like a man made hill overlooking the officer's mess with a mountain of concrete steps leading up to it.

The place was a tip inside it looked like no one had been in here for years. I found out later that this was a new duty for us and that we had never had to man the radio room before, it was something to do with the Vietnam War.

I reconnected the bank of batteries and connected them back to the mains so they were permanently charged, switched on the radio and tuned into the frequency I had been given, just general chatter between various bases around Hong Kong, so I set about cleaning the place.

There was a back room which was locked and no one seemed to know where the keys were so I broke the lock and entered another tip, a few filing cabinets, a locker and a bed. 'That may come in handy' I thought, after cleaning up I locked up and went to the NAAFI to buy a padlock and a bolt, the padlock went on the outside of the back room door and the bolt on the inside, from there I went to the stores and conned some extra bedding out of the store man, then I went back to the radio room and made the bed up, I now had a little home from home where I could escape to and avoid all kinds of unpleasant jobs, the only thing left to do now was to find a way to get Jeanie up here.

"Hey up" said Justin, entering the door.

"Fuck me, you made me jump" I said.

"I heard you had got this job, what the fuck you want it for?" he asked.

"Come here look", I said, opening the backroom door and pointed to the bed.

"You planning on living up here?" he asked.

"Not a bad idea, but think for a minute" I said.

He stood there looking puzzled then the penny dropped.

"Jeanie" he said.

"Jeanie" I repeated.

"You clever bastard why didn't I think of that" he said.

"All I have to do now is get her up here" I said.

"That's easy the bus stops outside the NAAFI, it never gets stopped either coming in or leaving the camp, just tell her you will meet her at the NAAFI, then walk between our block and Jali Dins, (Jali Dins was the camp tailor) up the track and come up the hill the back way, no one will see you, I've just come up that way myself" he explained.

"Show me" I said.

"Not yet the Sarn't Majors looking for extra men for the guard duty tonight, it's Saturday and I'm meeting Tammy that's why I'm skiving up here" he said.

"We'd better stay here then, I'm meeting Jeanie later we're going out for a meal then to the cinema and I don't want a guard duty either" I said.

"What's the film?" he asked.

"God knows, some Chinese crap in Mandarin with Cantonese sub titles as usual I suppose" I said.

"Trying to get a handle on a bit of Chinese culture eh!" said Justin.

"Culture my arse, I'll not be watching the film" I said.

"No you'll be getting your hand on a bit of Chinese pussy instead" he said, laughing.

"More than my hand, I hope" I replied.

"You've got no problem with Jeanie, she thinks the sun shines out of your arse" said Justin.

"Anyway where are you and Tammy going?" I asked.

"Same place as you probably, to see the ping, pong, ping, film" he replied, imitating Chinese singing and dancing "Ping, Pong, Ping, Wing, Ding, Dong", he continued while dancing around the room.

We managed to evade the Sarn't Major; the last we heard was that he had collared Rod for the guard duty.

We quickly got ready and caught the bus to Shaukiwan bus station, where we were meeting Tammy and Jeanie.

As we passed the guardroom Rod was stood outside being inspected by the guard commander.

"Not looking very pleased is he" I commented.

"Fuck him, it serves him right he should get out of the way quicker" said Justin.

We alighted from the bus and saw Tammy and Jeanie running towards us, Jeanie flung her arms around my neck and kissed me.

"You miss me?" she asked.

I was seeing her almost every day so how could I miss her.

"I only saw you yesterday" I said.

"I know, but I miss you" she replied, kissing me again.

There was a small group of teenage lads close by us, one of them made a comment, even though I couldn't speak the language I guessed it was an insult.

Jeanie said something to them and one of them started to argue with her, I stepped towards him.

"What's his problem, Jeanie?" I asked.

By this time Justin was at my side and the Chinese lads were squaring up to us.

"No, we go" said Jeanie.

"What did he say?" I asked, but neither Jeanie or Tammy answered my question, grabbing both Justin's and my arms they pulled us away but the lads started to follow us still shouting what can only have been insults judging from the tone of their voices.

"I'm getting pissed off with these wankers" said Justin.

"Fuck it, come on let's sort them out" I said.

Just as we were about to turn round and confront them, Jeanie ran towards them screaming in English.

"You leave my husband alone" she shouted, waving her hand in the air showing them a ring she was wearing, this seemed to stop them in their tracks.

"What the fuck is happening?" asked Justin, who hadn't taken much notice of what Jeanie had just done.

The leader of the group, well the one who had been making the gob walked towards me, I was getting ready to thump him when he held his hand.

"I sorry, we thought you were sailors taking our girls for prostitute" he said, and shook my hand.

"We very sorry sir" he added.

With that they turned their backs and walked away.

"Let me see you hand" I said to Jeanie.

She held her hand up and sure enough there was a ring on her finger.

"Christ, you're not married are you?" I asked

"No, don't be silly I go with you" she replied.

"Then what's with the ring?" I asked.

"To keep stupid Chinese boy from asking me for date" she answered.

"You don't like Chinese boys?" I asked.

"No, they idiots like them" she said, nodding towards the lads who were still walking away.

"Ok, if you're happy you wear the ring" I said.

We walked a little farther then out of the blue she said,

"Anyway Chinese boy no good at jig a jig, they go quick bang bang then gone no thought for girl, she get nothing".

I'm not sure if she was talking to me or just making an informed observation, either way I couldn't help but smile.

"What you smiling at?" she asked looking up at me.

"Your funny" I said, "You make me smile".

"You make me smile too" she replied.

I could hear Tammy explaining to Justin as they walked ahead of us, what Jeanie had just done, turning around Justin said,

"Did you have a nice wedding you two, thanks for the invite".

"We're not the only ones, are we Tammy" I said, seeing her take a ring out of her bag and slip on her finger.

"No" she said, showing Justin her hand.

"Oh very nice how much did that cost me" he said.

"Nothing it mine" said Tammy, not quite getting the joke.

OK, so we looked like married couples, so what, we acted like we were, and anyway you would be surprised just how much trouble those rings kept us out of.

"Where are we going Justin?" I asked.

"The pictures I think" he replied.

"Yes, we go to cinema then go for a meal, or you want meal first?" asked Tammy.

"I'm not that hungry" I said.

"OK, cinema it is then" said Justin.

The Shaukiwan Theatre was in a derelict state and was apparently due for demolition the following year, we sat in the very back row, well we would, wouldn't we, because of the darkness I couldn't see very much but once my eyes became accustom to it I could see there were no more than about a dozen people in there and that included the four of us. Justin and Tammy sat in the same row has us, but at the other end.

The film was the usual ping pong rubbish.

"What's it about?" I asked.

"Boy meet girl, fall in love, girl father no like boy, they run away, father look for them, boy is big Chinese Lord, they marry, live happily ever after" explained Jeanie.

"Seen one then and you've seen them all" I commented.

"You no like film?" she asked.

"It's not that I don't like it, it's that I don't understand it" I said.

"I teach you Chinese" she said.

'Me learn Chinese' I thought, I can speak English, gibberish and rubbish and it's taken me twenty years to learn that, so what chance have I got with Chinese.

I did eventually learn some Chinese, just enough to get by on, it was never a lot of use to me, except years later when I went for a night out in England. You know, you're on your way home and one of your mates says, "Let's go for a Chinese", I often wonder if the Chinese say 'Let's go for an English' and of course Jeanie always springs into my mind.

You enter the takeaway and order by numbers, there is always a little Chinese fella peeping around the corner of the kitchen door gibbering away in Chinese and laughing, then a different one will come to the door to have a look, then another. I would keep silent just to hear what they were saying, it was always something about the English being drunk or a comment about the girl you were with. I would then speak in Chinese to the person serving us about what the ones in the kitchen were saying. This always stopped them in their tracks, but strangely enough it seemed to make them happy, perhaps they were bored just talking to each other, the only drawback was I couldn't get out of the place, they wanted to talk and talk, but it had its compensations too, most of the time I got my meal for free.

Sat there kissing and cuddling Jeanie in the back row of the pictures, well that's what the back row is for, neither of us by now were bothered about the film. Jeanie took my hand away from her breast and placed it on her leg, I moved my hand up the inside of her thigh.

"Rub me" she whispered.

I glanced over towards where Justin and Tammy were sitting, in the darkness it looked like Tammy had her head in Justin's lap, was she giving him a blow job, I glanced again, Oh! My god, yes she was, and they didn't seem to care if anyone saw them. I was always lead to believe that the Chinese girls didn't like oral sex and that they thought it was disgusting and only the bar girls, gays and prostitute's did it. I can't remember where I heard it or even who told me, maybe it's not true, I know that Jeanie never offered to do it with me and was very upset on the one occasion I tried oral sex on her.

Jeanie moaned and squeezed her thighs together trapping my hand between them, after a few seconds she relaxed

"Rub more" she whispered.

"Inside" she whispered again.

So I slipped my hand down the waist band into the inside of her panties and gently started to rub her again, within seconds she moan again, shuddered and clamped my hand between her thighs forcing my fingers to slide up inside her.

'This girl should be in the Olympics, she could orgasm for China' I thought. 'What you do to me?" she asked, looking up at me and smiling.

Thinking she had probably had enough I removed my hand?

"No don't, you stay" she said, replacing my hand back in between her legs.

I glanced back over at Justin and Tammy.

Justin was now performing oral sex on Tammy and from where I was sitting to looked like she was enjoying it, with her head flung back over the back of the seat she was pushing her hips upwards with Justin's head firmly planted between her legs. Strange creature's these Chinese girl's.

The film ended and we left the building, I was carrying my jacket in front of me for obvious reasons".

"We go for meal now?" asked Tammy.

"No, we go home now" replied Jeanie.

"Home" said Justin, looking puzzled.

"Yes, we have a surprise for you, follow us", said Jeanie.

We set off walking, 'Thank god we're not going for a meal', I thought, 'I've just spent the last two hours with me hand up her skirt, how could I eat using that hand'.

We stopped outside a takeaway and Justin and Tammy went inside to order 'English'. After walking a few more yards we arrived at a block of flats, entering the building the girls took us upstairs, we stopped outside a flat door.

"We here" announced Jeanie, opening the door.

"Our new flat" she announced again.

"Your flat?" asked Justin.

"Yes, we only got a couple of days ago" answered Jeanie.

"You like?" asked Tammy, showing us around,

"That lounge, that kitchen, that Lily room, that Monica room, that Jeanie room, that bathroom and that my room", she said, dragging Justin into her room and trying to close the door behind them.

Justin pulled Tammy back into the lounge.

"OK, we eat first" said Tammy, and she and Justin disappeared into the kitchen.

"Hey up you lot" said a voice from the lounge.

"Fuck me, it's Frank" I said.

He was sat on the sofa with Lily, and sat in an armchair on her own was Monica.

"Rod's got guard duty" I said to her.

"Not bothered, he wanker anyway" she replied.

"She's dumped him" said Frank.

"Well, I'm not surprised he treats her like shit anyway" said Justin, from the kitchen.

"Never mind Monica we will find you another boyfriend" I said.

"I don't want one, you all dick heads" she replied.

Jeanie seemed to take offence at this and said something to her in Chinese; Monica stared at her then stomped off towards her room.

"Don't be like that with her she's upset" I said, looking at Jeanie. "How would you like it if I treated you like that?"

"Sorry" said Jeanie, grabbing Monica who was crying and giving her a hug. Looking back at me with tears in her eyes Jeanie said, "You make me feel ashamed".

"Come here you silly girls" I said, putting my arms around both of them.

"Why I never get good boy like you?" sobbed Monica.

I wasn't sure if the question was aimed at me or at Jeanie so I didn't answer.

"Give up! You'll make his head swell" commented Frank.

"He no big head, he just care" replied Jeanie.

"Food" said Justin, emerging from the kitchen.

We sat and ate our meal, then watch a bit of TV, which was about one level up from the cinema as far as entertainment was concerned.

I was sat on the sofa between Jeanie and Monica, who were leaning across me whispering to each other and giggling, and as usual I hadn't got a clue what they were talking about, but Lily and Tammy kept looking over at them and smiling. I had an arm around each of them and Jeanie didn't seem to object to the fact that I had my arm around another girl, maybe she was still feeling sorry for her, I was.

What time we going back to camp?" I asked, really hoping that we weren't.

"You not going back to camp, you stay" said Jeanie.

My wish came true.

"You heard the girl" said Justin, "We stay".

"Not you, you go back to camp" said Tammy, looking at Justin.

Justin lifted her up in his arms and plonked her back down in the chair.

"Bye then" he said.

She jumped up and grabbed him.

"No I only joking" she said.

"So am I" he said, picking her up again and sitting back down with her on his lap.

"Makes your radio room look like a dump Sarge" said Justin, looking around.

"What's he done to the radio room?" asked Frank.

"Wait while you see it, proper little shagging den" said Justin.

"A bit surplus to requirements now" I said.

"What shagging?" interrupted Jeanie, "You no jig a jig without me".

"See, I no jig a jig without her" I said, laughing.

"I go to bed" said Monica.

"We go to bed too" said Jeanie pulling me up off the sofa.

"Don't do anything I wouldn't do" commented Frank.

"We only going to hold hands, me good girl" said Jeanie.

"Yer! Right" said Frank, as he and Lily disappeared into their room.

We undressed and got into bed, this was actually the first time in my life I'd been in bed with any girl, all the other times had been on the beach or a knee trembler up against a wall with some girl back home in England. We made love for what seemed like ages and in every conceivable position known to man. 'Perhaps that's the wrong choice of words thank god she had a good supply of condoms'.

We lay quiet in each other's arms.

"Listen, someone's crying" I said.

"Monica" said Jeanie, getting out of bed and completely naked she left the room.

A few moments later she returned with the sobbing Monica who was dressed in only her panties.

"What are you doing? I asked, covering myself up with the sheet.

"She upset, she stay with us awhile" said Jeanie, lifting the corner of the sheet up to let Monica get in bed.

"Are you sure this is a good idea?" I asked.

"It ok, she not hurt you" replied Jeanie.

"It's not what she will do to me, it's what I might do to her" I said.

"You cheeky boy" she said.

"It's you that's invited her into bed, not me" I said,

"What wrong, you not like her?" asked Jeanie.

"Of course I like her" I said, not really knowing how to answer her.

"Then if she no mind, then I no mind" said Jeanie.

"You no mind?" asked Monica, looking at me.

"No, but are you two sure you want to do this?" I asked.

"Yes", said, Jeanie.

"Ha, Ha" said Monica, nodding her head.

What was I thinking of, was I really trying to talk them out of it, this is supposed to be every man's fantasy, isn't it, three in a bed.

Jeanie climbed back into bed, straddle me and I slipped inside her, Monica removed her panties and snuggled up beside us and getting hold of my hand she placed it between her legs.

"You rub me and fuck Jeanie, then we swap over" she said.

I did has I was told, while I rubbed her, Jeanie rocked herself backwards and forwards on me. I must admit it felt unreal at first fucking one girl while playing another.

"Is this what you two were giggling about on the sofa?" I asked.

"Yes" admitted Jeanie.

"You planned this" I said.

"Yes" said Monica.

'Shut up John', I said to myself, 'you're talking too much, just enjoy it'.

Jeanie came to orgasm and laid flat on top of me, I stopped rubbing Monica, held Jeanie tightly and rolled over with her onto her back while I was still inside her, she put her legs up around my back and I thrust into her until I came at the same time she squealed, shuddered and came herself, we lay there awhile, kissing.

"My turn now" said Monica.

In the heat of the moment I had almost forgotten about her.

"Give me a minute" I said, still panting I lifted myself up off Jeanie.

"No, not yet" said Jeanie, holding me inside her with her legs, I could feel my erection going down, so I finally lifted myself up off her, sitting on the edge of the bed I tried to put on a new condom.

"Give to me" said Monica, pointing to the condom.

"Come here" she said.

I got back in bed and laid beside her, she put her hand on my penis and rubbed me; while I continued to I rub her. I was soon ready again, and she slipped the condom onto my erection, I played with her until she had an orgasm then I tried to mounted her.

"No" she said, stopping me.

"This way" she said, has she turned over onto her hands and knees.

"Doggy style" I said.

"It better that way, get more in" she said, has I knelt between her legs and entered her from behind.

She pushed herself backwards onto me, I looked down at Jeanie, wondering why she wasn't asking me to play with her like I had done when we were the other way round she had fallen asleep.

Trying not to disturb her I pushed gently into Monica, then back, then in again she started moaning, which turned into shrieks and then into shouts.

"Fuck. Fuck. Fuck. Fuck" she shouted.

'Christ she's going to wake the whole bloody neighbourhood up', I thought.

"Fuck. Fuck. Fuck" she shouted continually has I thrust into her.

"Go on, ride her cowboy" said Jeanie.

"I thought you were asleep?" I gasped.

"Fuck. Fuck. Fuck. More. More. More" shouted Monica.

"You no jig a jig me like that?" said Jeanie.

"I do" I gasped again.

"You do me doggy next time" she said smiling.

"Fuck. Fuck. Fuck. Oh! Oh! Oh! You cum now" screamed Monica.

I thrust into her for all I was worth, as we came together she pushed backwards onto me and I leaned back and pushed my hips forward which gave even more penetration into her.

"Now" she screamed, her body went rigid as I let myself go into her.

We stayed in that position a little while before relaxing.

"Fuck me that was fantastic" I said.

"I have fuck you" said Monica, looking back at me over her shoulder has she dropped back onto all fours.

"Wow! Fuck me", I said again.

"Later" said both girls.

"Don't think I can again tonight girls" I said pulling out of Monica.

"If you want anymore you'll have to do it yourself" I said, jokingly.

My legs were aching, my back was aching, my heart was pounding like an express train and my poor old willy was all shrivelled up.

I lay down on the bed, Jeanie and Monica started to kiss and fondle each other, rubbing each other and rolling one on top of the other.

"Are you two lesbians now?" I asked.

"No we just good friends", said Jeanie, giggling.

I watched them for awhile, then I realised I was getting another erection.

"You ready again?" asked Monica, who was laid on top of Jeanie.

"Looks like it" I replied.

"Come here, I tell you what we do", said Monica, who was still lying on top of Jeanie.

"You kneel between our legs and you fuck us both together" she said.

They both opened their legs and I knelt between them.

"Yes" I said, thinking I knew what I was doing.

"You fuck me doggy then you fuck Jeanie and rub me then you fuck me doggy again, until we all cum, OK" she explained.

Now why didn't I think of that?

"OK" I said, "Who's first?"

"Take your pick you got two pussies to pick from" giggled Jeanie.

Jeanie spoke first so I entered her first, it was a bit of a problem with her being under Monica, but she positioned herself as to make it easier for me and I put my hands under her bum and lifted them both up.

While I was fucking Jeanie, the girls were kissing and fondling each other's breasts, this was really turning me on. I had never dreamed of doing it this way, well I wouldn't, this was the first time in my life I had been to bed with two girls at once.

"Fuck me now" said Monica rubbing her pussy against Jeanie and my cock has I went in and out.

I pulled out of Jeanie and entered Monica from behind.

"Wow! I like that, your balls bounce on my pussy when you fuck her" giggled Jeanie.

"Me again now" she demanded.

So doing as I was told, I pull out of Monica and back into Jeanie again.

They were both having orgasms has I went from one to the other and back again.

"Which one of us you cum in?" asked Jeanie.

"Which one of you wants it?" I asked.

"Me" said Monica looking back over her shoulder.

"Me too" said Jeanie.

"Then both it shall be" I said.

"How you going to do that, you only got one cock" laughed Jeanie.

"Wait and see" I said.

I started thrusting deeper into Jeanie, left her and thrust into Monica again, then back to Jeanie again, they were both screaming and moaning, I fucked them faster and faster until they and I were on the verge of cuming.

I was inside Jeanie and pushing my fingers into Monica, when Jeanie arched her back almost throwing Monica off her, she had cum first and at that moment so did I.

"Cum in me now" demanded Monica.

I thrust back into Monica just has she had another orgasm, pumping a few more times I came inside her.

We lay there in a big heap.

"You two bloody heavy" said Jeanie from the bottom of the heap.

"Sorry" I said and rolled off, followed by Monica.

See I told you, him good fuck" said Jeanie.

"Him better fuck than Rod, he no good fuck", replied Monica, gasping for breath.

As I lay there recovering I realised what Monica had just said, I was fucking Rod's ex girlfriend and not only that, I had my girlfriends permission to do so. 'It doesn't get much better than that John lad' I thought to myself.

Jeanie cuddled closer.

"Next time we do jig a jig sandwich I go in middle" she said.

"Where did you two learn that trick?" I asked.

"We no learn it we never do that before, that was first time we try it" answered Jeanie.

"So you two have been planning this?" I asked.

"Yes, we just needed you, to make up threesome" admitted Jeanie.

"So what else have you got planned?" I asked.

"You wait and see", she said.

"I think you two girls are trying to kill me?" I said.

"We fuck you to death, what a way to go" laughed Jeanie.

We must have fallen asleep, the next thing I remember is waking up, it was still dark outside and the girls were fast asleep. I needed a piss so very quietly I extracted myself from the tangle of arms and legs.

I sat on the edge of the bed and for a moment looking down at the two naked girls that I'd just spent the most fantastic night of my life with. They were both sleeping like babies and looked absolutely beautiful, what the hell was a prick like me doing with these two.

I opened the bathroom door and saw Justin and Tammy in there, they were both naked.

"Sorry" I said, backing out of the room.

"It's OK, come in" said Tammy.

"Sorry" I said again, "I didn't know anyone was in here you should lock the door, I need a pee".

They didn't seem to mind so I went about my business, then it dawned on me what they were doing. Tammy was giving Justin a Back, Crack and Sack wax to remove his body hair and that's when I saw it, Tammy had a penis, she's a male. 'Christ or bloody mighty' I thought. She hides that well, she looks, acts and to all intents and purposes is a woman, how the hell can a bloke look like she does, she certainly had me fooled.

I went back to the bedroom and sat back on the edge of the bed, looking down at the girls again, I looked at their private parts, why I don't know, perhaps to reassure myself that they were girls, 'Of course their girls, you daft twat, what are you thinking of' I said to myself.

Jeanie turned over and woke up, looking up at me sat on the edge of the bed.

"What you doing out of bed?" she asked.

"I needed the bathroom" I replied.

"You get back in bed, it not morning yet" she said, moving over to make room.

I got back in bed between her and Monica who was still fast asleep.

"Tammy and Justin were in the bathroom and ..."

She put her finger across my lips she knew what I was going to say.

"You see Tammy?" she asked.

"Yes" I replied.

"She my brother, she lady-boy, you not know, Justin no tell you?" she asked.

"No, I didn't know" I said.

"You no mind" she asked.

"I don't mind, it's got nothing to do with me, but you lot never cease to amaze me, one day I'm going to write a book about you" I said.

"Who me?" asked Jeanie.

"All of you" I replied.

"It be international bestseller" laughed Jeanie.

"Yer right, but I still don't understand why you two girls are sharing me?" I asked.

By now Monica was awake and listening to us.

"Because she my cousin and we like share" laughed Monica.

"She's your cousin" I asked, pointing to her.

"Yes" replied Monica.

"Well there's nothing like keeping it in the family, I'm definitely going to write that book" I commented.

So there I was with two Chinese cousins, one of whom had a gay transvestite brother, what a family, 'Perhaps we should rename Tammy,

Tommy, on second thoughts that may be his real name, don't ask' I thought.

"Are there any more members of your family around here that I don't know about?" I asked.

"No, just me Monica and Tammy" replied Jeanie.

"What about Lily" I asked.

"No, she just a friend", she replied.

"No, is she a girl?" I asked.

"Yes, you want me go get her, you find out" she said.

"I'm sure Frank would be pleased if you did that" I said.

"We go get Lily" she said.

"No, for god's sake no, I'm having a hard time just keeping up with you two, let alone three of you." I said.

"You give me hard time now" said Monica, turning over onto her hands and knees, once again kneeling between her legs I entered her from behind.

The next thing I knew was when I saw Frank stood in the doorway.

"You getting up today or what?" he asked.

"What time is it?" I asked.

"About twelve" he replied.

"What lunch time, twelve?" I asked.

"Yep! One, two, three", he said pointing his finger and counting.

"Three in a bed" he laughed.

"And the little one said" I continued.

"You randy little bastard, Sarge" he said.

"On your bike" I said, has he walked off down the passage towards the lounge, I could hear him telling the others, and a few moments later they were all at the door.

What's up with you lot, have you never seen three people in a bed before?" I asked.

They just stood there laughing, so jokingly I said,

"Now piss off, I got some serious jig a jiggin to do".

"You been jig a jiggin all night and kept us awake, now we know why" said Lily, looking at Jeanie.

"You want join us Lily?" asked Monica.

"Yer Lily, you come do foursome" laughed Jeanie.

For a second Lily hesitated and looked like she was going to accept the invitation, but before she had chance to say anything else Frank pulled her away , then they all left.

"And shut the fuckin door" I shouted after them.

"We do more jig a jig?" asked Monica.

"We do jig a jig sandwich one more time then we get up" said Jeanie.

"OK" I said, as Monica went to lie on top of Jeanie.

"No" said Jeanie. "It's my turn in the middle."

Monica didn't argue, they just swopped places, but unlike last time where Monica had kept her legs straight, Jeanie was on her knees with a leg either side of Monica's body squatting and laying on top of her at the same time, Jeanie's legs were now out of the way and this made it easier for Monica to open her legs wider and bend her knees, it also made it easier for me to penetrate them both.

"You start with me first this time" said Monica.

Positioning myself between Monica's legs, she pushed down with her feet on the bed lifting both her and Jeanie upwards towards me I slipped my cock into her and my fingers into Jeanie.

It was around 2pm when we finally emerged from the bedroom, the others were sat in the lounge.

"Where's Frank?" I asked.

"He's got guard duty tonight, so he's gone back to camp" explained Justin.

"Poor fucker pulling guard duty on a Sunday" I said.

"We all have to do it" said Justin.

"I'm in the shit when I get back anyway" I said.

"Why what you done?" asked Justin.

"It's what I've not done, I was supposed to make the 8am call to control in the radio room and I forgot all about it" I explained.

"I'm not surprised you forgot after what you got up to last night and anyway it's too fuckin late to worry about it now, so unless someone pulls you up about it, don't mention it" said Justin.

"I need a shower, I stink" I said.

"We no got shower but we go for bath" said Jeanie, linking my arm she walked me into the bathroom, where Monica was already in the bath.

"Move over" said Jeanie, throwing her dressing gown to the floor she climbed into the bath with Monica.

"What you waiting for?" she asked, looking up at me.

"There is no way all three of us are going to get in there" I said.

I knelt down beside the bath, picked up the soap, dipped it into the water and lathered it in my hands until they were covered in thick creamy bubbles. Justin's big yellow dildo sprang to mind, 'what I could do with that now' I thought.

"Why you laugh?" asked Jeanie.

"Oh nothing" I said, not realising I had laughed out loud.

"You get in bath now" said Jeanie.

"Lay back and relax", I said, rubbing my soapy hands on Jeanie's shoulders, moving down onto her breasts I felt her nipples harden, I moved my hands down her body then back to her breasts again.

"Oh! That nice" she said

I then did the same with Monica, caressing them both with my soapy hands.

"Oh! Yes" moaned Monica has I cupped her breast in my soapy hands and gentle squeezed her nipple.

"You get in bath now" said Jeanie.

How could I refuse, it was going to be a bit of a squeeze, but they sat up and I climbed into the bath between them.

Monica moved and sat on the end of the bath with her feet still in the water, I sat facing Jeanie with my back to Monica, who pulled me backwards and put her legs over my shoulders, the back of my head was now resting on her pussy.

"If I were the other way around" I said.

"I know, you lick, lick" replied Monica laughing.

I thought Chinese girls didn't like lick, lick", I said.

"Not sure, I never try lick, lick" she replied.

"You don't know what you're missing" I said trying to sit up with the intention of turning round to face her.

"No, you stay, lick, lick later" said Jeanie rubbing her soapy hands all over my legs and stomach while Monica did the same on my arms and chest.

I lay there being bathed by two girls, something akin to a Roman Emperor; all I was short of was the bunch of grapes.

I had an erection and Jeanie reached down and held me in her hand, then gently started to wank me, very slowly at first then getting a little faster and a little faster.

"No, stop" I said, removing her hand.

"You not like?" she asked.

"Yes I like, but you will make me cum in the bath if you carry on", I said.

"It no matter, I make you cum" she replied holding me again and moving her hand in a steady rhythm.

"I go get condom" said Monica, lifting her legs up off my shoulders.

"No" I said, holding her down with my hands on her thighs, I liked being there with my head resting on her pussy and Jeanie slowly wanking me, I didn't want to move.

"He cum soon" laughed Monica.

"How do you know?" I asked looking up at her.

"Bet he can hit you in the eye with cum" laughed Monica.

"I bet you he can't" replied Jeanie.

"Why?" asked Monica.

"I'm cuming" I shouted, as Jeanie moved her hand faster.

"Watch this" replied Jeanie, bending forwards and taking my cock in her mouth she sucked the last drop of spunk from me.

"Jeanie, What you doing?" shouted Monica."

"Oh! God, this fantastic, you try it Monica" said Jeanie.

"Maybe sometime" replied Monica, with a screwed up funny look on her face.

"We do something different now" said Jeanie, getting out of the bath and directing me to the other end away from Monica; she climbed back into the water facing me with her back to Monica and lay down.

"You fuck me this way" she said, indicating that I lay on top of her. I did as I was asked, this put me face first between Monica's thighs.

"You get lick, lick now Monica" said Jeanie.

"No, not want lick, lick" protested Monica putting her hands on her pussy.

"He not hurt you, you try, I did suck, suck, now you try lick, lick" said Jeanie.

"Ok" replied Monica reluctantly moving her hands.

"Don't you drown under there, will you?" I said, pumping into Jeanie while burying my face into Monica's pubic hair and tasting her wet pussy.

"Oh! Oh!" moaned Monica.

"See, I told you, you like" said Jeanie from underneath me.

"I need fuck now" moaned Monica.

"He fuck you and lick me now" said Jeanie, getting up to change places with Monica.

We stayed in the bath until the water started to cool, like three daft kids, having sex, playing, laughing, giggling and splashing in the water.

Justin and Tammy had gone out by the time we emerged from the bathroom. Lily was curled up on the sofa watching TV.

"You been long time" she said.

"You should have come in" said Monica.

"No, I go with Frank" she replied.

"We no tell Frank, him not know" said Monica.

Lily just said, "Maybe", and shrugged her shoulders.

Were they trying to convince Lily to have sex with me?

'Why' I thought.

Jeanie went into the kitchen to make coffee, Monica sat on the sofa next to Lily, they were chatting away to each other in Chinese and giggling, I understood parts of what they were saying because Jeanie had secretly been teaching me Chinese, Monica was telling her what we had got up to last night and in the bath.

Jeanie emerged from the kitchen carrying a tray with four pots of coffee on it, she had been listening to the other two and joined in the conversation.

Sat drinking my coffee I looked over at them, Jeanie was wearing just her dressing gown, and I knew she was naked underneath, Monica was in just her panties and Tee shirt with no bra, and Lily was wearing shorts and a Tee shirt, their hair which all three wore long was untidy, but to me they looked fantastic.

Jeanie turned to me and spoke in Chinese.

"Do you want to have sex with Lily?" she asked.

"What" I replied, a bit taken aback by the question.

Monica and Lily both jumped up in surprise.

"He understands you" exclaimed Monica.

"Yes, I know he does" replied Jeanie.

"You should have told us" said Lily.

"That's not fair" said Monica.

"It's not fair when you speak Chinese and he can't understand you, is it" said Jeanie.

"Well do you?" asked Jeanie again, looking back at me.

'Are you daft woman of course I want sex with Lily, she's gorgeous, which bloke in their right mind wouldn't' I thought to myself.

I looked directly at Lily,

"Do you want to have sex with me?" I asked

"Yes she does" said Monica.

"Let her answer for herself" I said.

"No" replied Lily blushing.

"Because of Frank" I asked.

We won't tell him, if you don't tell him" said Monica.

"Look, she doesn't want to, now leave her alone" I said

Lily got up off the sofa, walked across the room towards me, kissed me on the cheek and smiled.

We stayed in the flat for the rest of the day, at bedtime Jeanie took me back to her room and Monica followed, and once again we had sex for most of the night.

It was about 6 am the next morning when Justin put his head around the bedroom door and woke me.

"Come on, Sarge we have to get back to camp" he said.

Before I had chance to reply he looked at us on the bed.

"Fuck me, you still doing threesomes?" he asked.

"Looks like it" I said, looking back at the sleeping girls.

"Where you go?" asked Jeanie, rubbing her eyes.

"Back to camp, we're on duty in two hours, I'll see you later" I replied.

"OK, bye" she said, and lay back down.

I went to the radio room while the rest of the platoon went on the 8am parade. After making the morning call I stayed there trying to keep myself busy, in reality I was skiving, putting some paperwork away in the cabinet and with my back to the door.

"Morning Private Sargeant" said Capt Red.

Christ, I hadn't seen him coming up the steps.

"Morning Sir" I replied.

"Everything OK?" he asked, picking up the logbook and reading through it.

"Yes Sir, no problems".

"Anything I need to know about?" he asked.

"No Sir" I replied.

"Well I'm glad to see you haven't booked any imaginary calls to control" he said.

'Oh! Christ he knows I missed a call' I thought.

At that moment Justin walked in.

"Fuck me" he said, when he saw Capt Red was there.

"No thank you Sidebottom, I'll give it a miss if you don't mind and what are you doing here?" he asked.

"Just come to get Sarge Sir, we have to report to the signals stores" replied Justin.

This seemed to take his mind away from the missed call he had come to see me about.

"Go on then, get yourselves off to the stores and don't be skiving up here all day" he said, leaving the room.

"Do we really have to report to the stores?" I asked.

"Yep" said Justin.

"I fuckin hate that place, we'll be there all day cleaning every bit of equipment there is" I said.

"Come on the sooner we get there the sooner we will be finished" said Justin.

Walking down to the stores we talked about the girls and I mentioned that I knew about Tammy's little secret, which didn't seem to cause him any concern, so I left it at that.

We had to pass the outdoor swimming pool to get to the stores where some of the family men were in the pool with their wives and kids. One young girl in a yellow bikini was on the edge of the pool on her hands and knees talking to someone in the water, with her bum facing towards us.

"How about that for a back scuttle" I said.

"Remind you of anyone?" asked Justin.

"Yer" I replied, as a vision of Monica flashed into my mind.

"You randy bastard, don't you ever think of anything else" said Justin.

"What else is there?" I asked.

"Come, let's get on" he said.

"Aye, on her" I said, looking back at the young girl at the pool side.

"Give up she's not old enough and anyway her dad will fucking kill you" said Justin.

Why, who's her dad" I asked.

"One of the Sarn't Majors" he replied.

Then I reminded him about Randy Mandy in Cyprus.

"Yer right" he said, laughing.

Half of the platoon was at the stores when we arrived.

We were met by 'Raggy' our platoon Sergeant,

"Where the fuck you two been?" he asked, and without waiting for a reply, said,

"Right my bonny lads, we're getting all new equipment later today, so the old stuffs got to be cleaned and packed away ready for shipment back to the UK".

'Oh! No we'll be here all day' I said to myself.

"Sargeant, you listening to me" he shouted.

My mind was still on the girl in the yellow bikini, glancing across at her still knelt by the pool.

"No good looking at her you dirty pervert she's only fifteen" he said.

"Fifteen fuck me, they didn't make them like that when I was fifteen" I said.

"Get to fuckin work" snapped Raggy, shaking his head from side to side and walking away.

We cleaned and boxed equipment for the next couple of hours.

"NAAFI break" shouted Raggy, "and I want you back here in half a hour, no fuckin skiving off, or else".

I still couldn't keep my eyes off the girl by the pool.

'Fifteen' I kept thinking, she's got bigger tits than Jeanie and Monica put together 'How can she only be fifteen'.

"For fucks sake, get your eyes off her" said Justin.

"I can't help it, she's fuckin gorgeous" I said.

"Aye and she's underage" said justin.

"If their old enough to bleed, then their old enough to butcher" said Midnight, who had been stood behind us listening to our conversation.

"Your worse than him" said Justin.

"Maybe, but she is a good looking lass even if she is too young" replied Midnight.

"Just think what she's going look like in a few years time" I said.

"Come on, before tha gets a hard on and wants to go for a wank lets get to the NAAFI" said Justin.

We had to pass the pool again to get to the NAAFI.

"Look at that one in the pool" I said, spotting a girl in a black bikini, "Now don't tell me she's only fifteen".

"No she's eighteen the wife of a Corporal in 'C' company" said Justin.

"You want to get yourself on Lifeguard duty" said Midnight.

"What's that?" I asked.

"See those two lads over there" he said, pointing to some lads sat on chairs at the side of the pool, "Their on Lifeguard duty, it's like guard duties but the scenery better to look at, the only problem is your are not allow in the pool while you're on duty unless your rescuing someone".

"So I've got to jump in without being seen, drown her, then save her before I can fuck her" I said.

"Summit like that", laughed Midnight.

Anyway where you been Midnight, I've not seen you for ages" I asked.

"It's you that keeps going missing not me" he replied.

He was right, I was hardly ever in the barrack room these days, most of the time I kipping down in the radio room or at the flat with Monica and Jeanie.

He explained that he was now in the battalion rugby team and he was due to go on a NCO's cardre next week.

Sat in the NAAFI having a cuppa and a meat pie, I was looking around when I thought, 'I know that face, fuck me it's Billy Blow Job'.

"Billy Blow Job" I shouted.

"Who the fuck is Billy Blow Job?" asked Midnight.

"Sounds like my kind of guy" commented Justin.

Billy stood up and looked towards us.

"Fuckin hell Sarge it's you" he shouted.

Come over here and sit with us" I shouted back.

He joined us at our table and explained that he had waited until he was eighteen to join up, he was in 'One' platoon, 'A' company at the moment and wasn't too keen on it. I told him to go for the next signal cardre and apply to join the signal platoon. He did, because six weeks later he joined us.

We talked about old times before we joined up and about what had happened to each of us since.

"Let's get back to the stores" said Justin, interrupting us.

"Yer, I suppose your right" I said reluctantly agreeing with him.

"I'll see you later" I said to Billy.

Walking back past the pool, the girl in the yellow bikini had gone, feeling a little disappointed, I thought 'Ah well never mind, she's was too young anyway'.

"Fuckin late again you lot" said Raggy as we arrived back at the stores.

"I've got to go and see the CO so no skiving off while I'm gone" he said.

We were finishing up the last of the packing when Raggy returned.

"The new equipments not arriving while tomorrow now so you can go, but before you do mark the boxes U stroke S so we know it's duff kit", he said, then he left.

(U / S in the British army meant that the equipment was either old or faulty, U/S = useless.) In our rush to get away we missed the stroke out and marked the boxes 'US', a mistake that would later come back and bite us on the arse.

It was about 6pm when Justin and I finally arrived at the girls flat.

"Hi" I shouted.

"Where you two been?" asked Frank.

"I see you managed to get out of doing any work" said Justin.

"You two working, that's a first" laughed Frank.

Jeanie and Monica appeared from Monica's room when they heard us.

"Where you been" asked Monica.

"Working" I replied.

"You late" said Jeanie.

"Why, have you two started without me" I said, pointing to Monica's room.

"No, you silly, we wait for you" said Monica.

"Looks like another good night for you Sarge" said Frank.

"Yer, but it's fuckin me up trying to keep up with the two of them" I said.

"Get Monica off with yer new friend then" said Justin.

"Who's his new friend?" asked Frank.

"Billy Blow Job" replied Justin.

"Billy fuckin who job" said Frank laughing.

"He's an old mate from civi street, we were joining up together and he got knocked back, but he's now in 'A' company" I explained.

"Who Billy?" asked Jeanie.

"A mate of mine" I said.

"What he like?" asked Monica.

"He's very quiet and shy" I lied, "If you want to meet him I'll bring him with me next time".

"OK, he sound nice boy you bring him" said Monica.

We went to sit in the lounge where Tammy and Lily were sat eating.

"Hi you two" I said.

"Hi" said Tammy.

Lily looked up at me and smiled,

"Hello" she said,

We had a meal and sat with the girls on our laps, or in my case two girls on my lap we talked mainly about Billy for most of the evening. Eventually we drifted off to our respective bedrooms. I had an idea that this could be my last night with Monica so I made the most of it.

When the lads were skint and couldn't afford to go to the NAAFI, they could tick a couple of sandwiches and a mug of coffee while payday, from a little Chinese guy who we called Eggy. He had a small trolley with a tin box on one end filled with sarnie's, cakes and pies and two large urns on the other end filled with tea and coffee.

His pitch was directly outside our barrack block, we knew when he was there because he would shout, "Cheesy anniesannie" (Cheese and Onion Sandwich) in his best broken English.

There was also another sandwich man called Johnny he had the same sort of set up but on an old delivery bicycle, his sarnie's were in the basket and the urns strapped either side of the back wheel, his pitch was farther down the road outside 'A' company block.

One day Rod went to tick off Eggy, but he wouldn't let him have anything, he said he still owed him money.

He then tried to tick off Johnny, who also refused him because he knew that Rod owed money to Eggy.

Then Rod tried to get me, Justin and Frank to lend him something, Frank gave him one of his sarnie's.

"No way" said Justin.

"I can't it's our turn to buy in the shopping in for the girls" I said.

"Fuck the girls shopping" he said.

"Come on Rod be fair, we eat their food so it's only right we buy some back" said Frank.

"Arrrh! Fuck yer, yer wankers, I'll get my own back on those two bastards" said Rod, pointing at Eggy, and then down the road towards Johnny, with that he stormed back into the barrack block.

"What the fucks he up to?" asked Justin.

"Fuck knows, let's follow him and find out" I said.

We found him filling a condom with water in the bath.

"What you doing with that?" I asked.

"I'm going to water bomb the little bastard" he replied.

The condom was by now about two feet long and a foot wide laid in the bottom of the bath.

"How the fuck you going to move that?" asked Justin.

"Watch" replied Rod, running back to the barrack room, he returned a few seconds later with a blanket.

He worked the blanket under the condom.

"Get hold of a corner each" he said.

"Fuck off, I don't want owt to do with it" said Justin.

"Me neither" said Frank.

"Fuck off then yer twats, I'll do it myself" he said.

Rod strained and struggled but could barely lift it.

"For fucks sake, you'll give yourself a rupture" said Justin, grabbing a corner of the blanket.

I grabbed another corner and Frank grabbed the last one and together we lifted it out of the bath.

"Right come on, up to the roof" said Rod.

"Oh no, that's far enough" said Justin.

"Come on you've already got hold of it, let's get it up to the roof" said Rod.

The roof of the barrack blocks were flat with a normal stairway leading up to them, there was a wall about four feet high running around the edge.

We managed to get the water bomb up there and laid it down while Rod crept to the edge and looked over the wall.

"That way a bit" he said, lining it up with Eggy.

"Right are you ready" he said.

"One", we pulled the corners of the blanket upwards.

"Two", we pulled again.

"Three", and with an almighty tug we launched the water bomb condom towards Eggy.

It wobbled through the air from side to side like a giant jelly and burst as it landed smack bang in the centre of Eggy's sandwich box.

"What a fuckin shot" said Rod, looking back over the wall.

We heard Eggy screaming "I tell company commander".

Then we heard him run into the barrack block still screaming "I tell company commander".

"Fuck me he's got a fuckin great carving knife" said Rod.

"Fuck you I'm off" said Justin, and ran towards the back wall, took one leap onto the top of it and jumped.

"Where the fuck has he gone? I asked "We're four floors up".

"I'm going with him" said Frank.

"And me" said Rod, and they both ran towards the wall and jumped.

I followed, stopped and looked over the side, there was about a forty foot drop to the ground and no sign of the other three, then it darned on me they must have jumped onto the hill behind the block which was about a twenty feet away, 'I'll never clear that' I thought.

Then I heard Eggy getting closer, I backed up and ran.

'Arrrrgh you crazy bastard John' I said to myself, and jumped, landing on the other side like a sack of spuds,

I picked myself up and ran like hell in the direction of the radio room. The others were waiting for me out of sight behind the building.

"You got the keys?" asked Justin.

"Yep" I replied.

"Get the fuckin place open then" he said.

Once inside I locked the door and we hid in the backroom.

"Look at us, big rough tough soldiers running away from a little Chinese bloke with a carving knife" I said.

"Yer, too right" said Rod, "he'll fuckin kill us".

"We're gonna get some right shit for this if anyone saw us" said Frank.

"If we stay here awhile, we should be OK" said Justin.

After what seemed like eternity, but in reality was no more than a few minutes there was someone knocking on the outer door?

"Don't answer it" said Rod.

The knocking was getting louder, more frequent and more inpatient.

"Keep quiet and they'll probably go away" said Frank.

"Go and answer it Sarge, but don't tell them that we're in here" said Rod.

"Don't be so fuckin daft" I said, "What am I going to say when they ask me why I'm in here at this time of day".

"Sarge, if you're in there let me in" shouted Billy.

"It's Billy Blow Job" said Rod, "Quick let him in".

I unlocked the door grabbed him and dragged him inside.

"All hells broke loose down there" he said.

"Why what's happened?" asked Rod looking all innocent.

"Fuck off yer daft twat, you've just water bombed Eggy" he replied.

"How do you know?" I said.

"I followed Eggy up onto the roof and saw Sarge jump, he explained.

"Did Eggy see me?" I asked.

"Don't think so, he went straight to the front edge and had his back to you" he said.

"Thank fuck for that" I said.

"What's happening down there?" asked Justin.

"The Company Sar'nt Major and Raggy are running round like blue arsed flies and questioning everyone in the block to see if they know anything about it" he said.

"You can't stop here, if they find out its Sarge this is the first place they'll look" said Billy.

"Yer, your right, but where we gonna go?" asked Frank.

"I know, let's go over the back of the hill to bypass guardroom, walk down the road to Stanley and catch the bus to Shaukiwan and go to the girls flat, then tomorrow when we get back and they asks us where we were, we weren't even on camp, so they can't blame us" explained Justin.

"What about me?" asked Rod, "I can't go to the flat?"

"You stay in Stanley for awhile then return to camp as if nothing had happened" said Justin.

"I can't stay in Stanley, I've got no money" said Rod.

"You never have" commented Frank.

"Well go back down the hill around Jali Dins, across the road and into the NAAFI and pretend you've been in there all afternoon" said Justin.

"I can't go to the NAAFI what if someone already in there says I haven't been there all afternoon and anyway I've still got no money to go there with" he said.

"Here for fucks sake, now piss off and stop coming up with excuses, it's your fault we're in this shit it was your idea anyway." I said, handing him a ten dollar note.

"And I want it back on payday".

"And don't tell anyone about what we've done" said Frank, has Rod went out of the door.

"He's a wanker" said Justin.

"What about me?" said Billy, "I've got to get back to the barrack room without anyone seeing me and asking where I've been".

"You're coming with us" I said.

I had already explained to him all about the girls and that Monica wanted to meet him.

"I'm not dressed to go anywhere" said Billy, stood there in just a pair of old tatty shorts.

"Well we're not exactly dressed for man of the year are we, look don't worry we've got some clothes you can borrow once we get there" I replied.

"You won't have your clothes on for long anyway if Monica has anything to do with it", commented Frank.

"Is she that good?" asked Billy.

"Depends on your definition of good" replied Frank.

"Ask Sarge, he's the one that's been fucking her silly for the last three months" said Justin.

"He knows all about it" I said.

So we set off to make our way to Shaukiwan and the girls.

"Don't forget what I told you", I said to Billy, has we were going up the steps into the girls flat.

"Remind me again" he said.

"Look, just treat her with some respect and treat her gentle" I said, "Oh! And always use a condom.

"Just be nice to her" said Justin.

"Hi girls" shouted Justin, has we entered the flat.

"Hi" came four voices from the direction of the lounge.

"Monica, I've brought someone to see you" I shouted.

She came skipping up the corridor towards us like a two year old, flung her arms around my neck and kissed me.

"Not me, him" I said, pointing to Billy.

"Hi", she said to Billy smiling.

"Monica meet Billy, Billy meet Monica" I said.

"Hi" said Billy, a bit red faced has Monica kissed him on the cheek.

We walked into the lounge and settled down with our respective partners.

Billy sat in the armchair and Monica sat on the chair arm next to him with her arm around his shoulder, chatting and getting to know each other.

I sat with Jeanie on my lap, looking over at them, was I really feeling a bit jealous, had I become that much attached to Monica, that I felt uneasy watching her with another man, what was wrong with me.

Jeanie must have sensed there was something wrong she lifted my head up and turned it towards her.

"You ok" she whispered.

"I'm ok" I said, and kissed her.

"You going to miss Monica" she whispered again.

"Yes, but don't ask me why, I don't know" I admitted.

She smiled and kissed me again.

"I know why" she whispered in my ear again,

"Don't worry, she still share sometime".

For the rest of the evening I pretended not to care, but every time I saw them kissing or touching each other, I felt a little twinge of regret.

Frank was telling Lily what we had done and how we had escaped from camp. Lily laughed.

Things looked to be getting very intimate between Monica and Billy, she was now sat on his lap and every few seconds they were kissing, at one point I saw her move his hand onto her thigh.

"Take him into your room" said Jeanie in Chinese to her.

Billy clearly didn't understand what Jeanie had just said.

Monica nodded looked across at me, took Billy's hand and lead him to her room.

"Come on" Jeanie said to me, pulling me up off the sofa,

"We go to bed".

In bed with Jeanie I could hear Monica in the other room,

'Fuck. Fuck. Fuck', Billy had obviously made a good impression on her, and was certainly doing so now.

'Noisy little bugger' I thought, 'No wonder the rest of the flat knew what we were doing'.

"You should not get too attached, this only fun" she said.

"I know, but it doesn't stop me caring about you or Monica, does it" I replied.

"I know it difficult and we care for you too" she said.

Between sleep and sex with Jeanie, I laid awake listening to Monica and Billy for most of the night, until Justin put his head around the bedroom door at 6am.

It was time to return back to camp.

On the way back Justin asked Billy if he had, had a good night, Billy just said he had enjoyed it and that he thought Monica was a fantastic girl. Didn't we all.

I really didn't want to hear any of it, but I remained composed and didn't let it show.

We discussed what we were going to say if questioned about the water bomb.

We were ask by Raggy if we knew anything about it and told him no, because we weren't even in camp when it happened. I think he believe us but to make sure

Justin offered him Tammy's phone number and address so he could check for himself if he wanted to. This seemed to satisfy him and he left it at that.

Walking back to the barrack room one evening I past one of the lads who was giving a girl one, up against the wall at the side of the NAAFI.

'I know her' I thought,

'Fuck me it's yellow bikini girl from the pool'.

"What you looking at?" the lad asked.

"Yer, do know she's only fifteen, don't yer?" I said.

"Fuck it - I - don't - care - how – old –she - is" he panted, while banging away into her.

"I'm sixteen, it was my birthday last week" she gasped.

"Well, happy - fuckin - birthday - to - you" he panted, while continuing to bang away at her.

"Yer will care if the Sarn't Major finds out" I chuckled, and started to walk away.

"What the fucks it got to do with him?" he asked.

"You're fucking his daughter" I replied.

"I know I am, that's why I'm fucking her to get my own back on the bastard and anyway it's too fuckin late noooooow" he groaned.

"That was quick" moaned yellow bikini girl as the lad pulled out of her and walked away.

"Your funeral" I said, and continued to walk towards my barrack block.

"Don't go" she said, "Don't you want to fuck me now?"

"You'd better get him to do it again love, I'm not touching you, your jail bait" I said, still walking away.

Not like me to turn down a fuck, but knowing who her dad was I suppose you have to draw the line somewhere.

What is it about Sarn't Major's daughters that make them want to be fucked by every soldier on camp, perhaps it's a way for them to get their own back on their Dads?

"Come on, don't be a spoilsport, my Dad will never find out" she said following me and grabbing my hand to pull me back.

"He'd better not" I said leading her around the other side of the Naafi where the outside trestle tables were located. She pulled me towards her up against the wall. I kissed her and caressed her body, her nipples hardened to my touch, pulling her dress up around her waist I put my hand between her legs and onto the inside of her panties, her pubic hair and cunt was still wet from the last lad, pushing my fingers inside her she moaned and let the full weight of her body rest on my hand, her juices ran down the inside of her thighs.

"Fuck me" she whispered.

I pulled her away from the wall towards one of the tables and bent her forwards over it, lifted her dress up over her buttocks, pulling her pants halfway down her thighs I spread her legs and pushed my fingers once more into her wet pussy from behind while I released my cock from the confines of my shorts.

"Finger me in my bum and cunt at the same time" she whispered.

I push my fingers into both her holes and she moaned out loud, in fact so loud I thought someone must surly hear us.

"Fuck me in my bum" she whispered.

Without saying a word I did as she asked and push my cock into her arse. I had never bum fucked a girl before and was surprised at her request and how easy it was to enter her. Pumping into her; I could feel her rubbing her cunt at the same time.

"In my cunt now" she demanded.

Once again I did as I was asked, sliding in and out of her, from one hole to the next and back again.

"Harder, I'm cumming" she demanded, shuddering with the force of her orgasm.

I pulled out of her cunt and pushed into her bum, a few seconds later I shot my load inside her. I didn't want to cum inside her cunt; I wasn't wearing a condom and didn't want to be the one responsible if she got pregnant, besides I'd never cum up a bum hole before.

"You filled my bum with spunk" she almost shouted out with glee.

I pulled out of her and my spunk followed me, it trickled down her crack onto her still open cunt, she reached between her legs and retrieved some on her fingers then put her fingers in her mouth sucking them and tasting me.

"Now go home and stop playing grownups" I said slapping her on the bum, pulling up my shorts and walking away.

"See you again sometime and thanks" she replied pulling up her panties.

"Anyone want a fuck?" I asked, entering the barrack room.

"Why, you offering?" asked Justin.

"The Sarn't Major's daughter is, she's just asked me if I want to" I said.

"Who yellow bikini girl?" asked Justin.

"Yep" I replied.

"Where is she?" asked Rod, "I'll fuck her".

"Side of the NAAFI, she just had one lad and is looking for another, she wants more" I said.

Rod jumped off his bed and ran out of the room.

"He'll get locked up, that daft bastard, if he gets caught with her" said Justin.

"His problem" I said.

"Did she really ask you to fuck her?" asked Frank.

"Yep, the other lad had no sooner shot his bolt, when she asked me if I wanted to take his place".

"And you refused" said Frank.

"Too right I did, she's the Sarn't Major's daughter" I said not wanting to admit that I had just fucked her.

Rod came back into the room looking disappointed.

"You lying bastard she's not there" he said.

"Ok, then don't believe me" I said.

I walked out of the door and looked over towards the NAAFI.

"She's there" I said, pointing towards the grass bank at the side of the square.

The others came to have a look.

"There look" I pointed, "On the grass".

"Yer, your right" said Justin.

"I'm going to wait my turn" said Rod, setting off down the stairs and out across the square towards them.

"I'll be back in a minute" said Justin.

"Why are you going to shag her as well?" asked Frank.

Justin returned with a pair of binoculars and put them up to his eyes.

"What's happening?" I asked.

"The other lads done and is walking away" he said.

"What's Rod doing?" asked Frank.

"He's talking to her, no hang on, he's laid on the grass next to her, now he's on top of her.

The runners and riders are at the post and their off, it's fanny wide open with cock cuming up the centre and two legs on the outside, there's thrusting on the inside and vinegar stoke not far behind, their coming up to the big jump now and cock is the winner by a good six inch", said Justin, as if he were commentating on a horse race.

I was still laughing when I noticed Frank was missing,

'Don't tell me he's gone to fuck her now' I thought.

"Where's Frank?" I asked.

"He's photographing the winner" said Justin.

Frank had grabbed a camera and had used nearly a full roll of film taking pictures of them while they were shagging.

Rod chased Frank back to the block when he realised what he had been doing.

"You bastard" he shouted after him, leaving poor yellow bikini girl on the grass with her legs still wide apart, looking like she was waiting for her next customer.

"You bastard, gimme that fuckin camera" shouted Rod, chasing Frank back to the barrack room.

"Fuck off tha not having it" said Frank.

"What's tha gonna do with it" demanded Rod.

"Gonna have them developed and sell them around camp" laughed Frank.

"Tha can't, NAAFI won't develop them" said Rod.

"Who says I'm taking them to the NAAFI, I know a lad in admin who will do it for me if I let him keep a couple of the best ones", said Frank, removing the film from the camera.

"Bastard" said Rod, trying to grab the film.

"In fact I'm going to see him now" he said, leaving the room.

Frank was gone for about three hours, we thought he may have got way laid by yellow bikini girl, laid being the operative word, eventually he returned clutching a handful of photo's.

"Some are Ok, some are crap and some didn't even come out, but this one's a beauty" he said, thumbing through them and waving one under Rod's nose.

Rod jumped up grabbed it and looked at it.

"It's blank" he said, ripping it in two.

"This one's not though" said Frank, passing it to me.

"That's a cracker, look at this Justin" I said passing it to him.

"Oh, very artistic, excellent piece of workmanship" commented Justin.

"What's that on your arse?" he asked.

"It's his war wound" said Frank.

"Could have done with maybe a little more makeup to cut down on the shine" said Justin.

"On this one you can actually see who it is" said Frank, passing another photo to me.

"This is the one for the notice board" I said, trying to pass it to Justin, while Rod was jumping up and down in between us trying to grab it.

The other photos were body on body with some showing yellow bikini's face but not Rod's, and some of them were cock in pussy close ups.

Rod managed to get hold of a couple of them and rip them up, but Frank just pulled extra copies out of his pocket.

"The lad in admin has got plenty more copies if we need them" said Frank, taking the piss.

Rod finally calmed down and we agreed to destroy the one's that could identify him, if he agreed to stop ripping them up.

He thumbed through them, turning them round and looking at them from different angles, while making various comments about his performance.

The next morning someone had pinned one of the photos showing yellow bikini's face and one of the close ups just to prove that penetration had taken place on the notice board in the NAAFI. Rod played fuckin hell up with us, but we had nothing to do with it, it must have been the lad from admin.

At NAAFI break there was a large crowd gathered around the board, everyone wanted to know how they could get hold of a copy, it quickly became classified as official wanking material by the lads and copies were pinned to the back of every toilet door on the camp.

Word must have got around fast because the Sarn't Major came storming into the NAAFI, looked at the photos of his daughter being fucked, ripped them off the board and stormed back out again without saying a word.

The next thing we knew, was that there was to be a full camp search for more copies and everyone's locker got turned out, they found some but the more they found the more we printed, we stopped the lad in admin from printing them it was getting too risky, so we took them down town and had them done there, some even found the way into the Wan Chai bars, the negatives were never found I had them stashed away in the radio room.

There was also a rumour going round that the Sarn't Major wanted to have an arse identity parade so he could find out which of the lads it was. Rod was shitting himself.

Copies of the photos kept cropping up all over the camp for months afterwards, we were warned that anyone caught in possession of one would face a Court Marshall, and if it were proved that it was their arse in the photo they would be charged with rape.

How they were going to prove whose arse it was is still a mystery, unless they were hoping to find Rod's war wound, which was a very small scar on his left buttock.

We didn't see yellow bikini girl around camp for a long time after that, which was a shame because she was a good looking girl.

I suppose she probably got grounded.

There was to be a big dance, or 'Ball' has the officers called it, in the officer's mess one night and Raggy Tash was patrolling the barrack room during the day trying to get some of the lads to be waiters for the night.

"It's a great job" said Justin.

"I've done it before" said Frank.

"Yer you get free booze and goodies" said Justin.

"Well yer not supposed to, but as long as you don't get caught nicking it, who knows" said Frank.

"There are also some nice posh girls there so come on lets go for it" he said.

"No, I don't fancy it" I said, "I'm getting out of the way" and with that I went up to the radio room.

I must have fallen asleep on the bed, it was dark when I woke up, I was about to lock up and go back to the barrack room when I heard the music coming from across the road and remembered about the ball in the officers mess.

Sitting at the desk I watched through the window and saw Justin and Frank along with a few of the other lads dressed like penguins prancing about with trays in their hands serving drinks to the officers in their full dress uniforms and their ladies in evening gowns.

'Posh gits' I thought, 'What some of those girls need is a bit of rough'.
Was I now wishing I was down there with them?
'No don't be daft'.
I don't know how long I sat watching, it didn't really matter I had nowhere to go. Justin and Frank were working, Billy was out somewhere with Monica, probably back at the flat with Jeanie, and trying to get Lily to join in, like Jeanie had said 'It only fun'.
So why was I sitting here why wasn't I with Jeanie? To be honest I don't know, perhaps I needed to be on my own and away from her for a little while.

The door flew open, banged against the wall and I nearly fell out of my chair with the shock. Stood in the doorway was a girl wearing a blue low cut evening gown which was even lower back and didn't leave very much to the imagination, one strap kept falling off her shoulder revealing her breast, carrying her shoes in one hand, an empty glass in the other with the remains of her once immaculate hair style falling down.
"Hello, what do you do in here? She asked, slurring her words, she had obviously had too much to drink.
"It's where I work" I replied.
"Oh! Work, how boring" she said.
Have you lost your way?" I asked, trying to be polite.
"No the grownups are boring the pants off me down there, I just had to get out" she said.
She staggered towards the backroom.
"Got any drinkies?" she asked.
I did have a few bottles of San Mig in one of the lockers, but I wasn't about to offer her one of them, she had drunk enough already by the looks of her.
"No sorry" I said.
"Oh! Bugger, no drinkies, I'll go and get some" she said, stumbling back out of the door.
I watched her through the window wobbling her way down the steps and back to the officer's mess.
'Christ, she'll break her silly neck if she falls down there'
'I wonder if she will come back, no don't be daft John' I thought.
I continued to watch her until she disappeared into the mess, and then went back to my daydreaming,
I noticed she had left her shoes behind. I couldn't take them back to her in the mess, what reason would I have for having her shoes, picking them up I took them into the backroom and hid them. On returning to the front office, there she was again, this time carrying a half empty champagne bottle and a tray of food.
"Got any glasses" she asked.
"No sorry" I replied.

"Never mind it doesn't matter" she said, taking a swig from the bottle and spilling most of its contents down her breasts.

"Have a drinkie" she said, passing the bottle to me.

I took it from her, put it to my lips and pretended to have a drink.

I was still in the doorway of the backroom when she stumbled towards me and put her free arm around my neck, nearly dropping the food.

I was trying to hold her up, balance the tray and keep hold of the bottle all at the same time, so I sat her on the edge of the bed, as I did so, both her shoulder straps fell down revealing her breasts, she was now naked from the waist up, I turned away to put the tray and bottle down, on turning back towards her, she was laid on the bed, making no attempt to cover herself.

"Your breasts are out, do you know?" I asked, 'Now that has got to have been the most stupid question I have ever asked a girl in my life'.

"Yes" she replied, taking one in each hand and squeezing them together.

"They're nice aren't they, have a feel" she said, waggling her tits at me.

"I assume you're one of the officer's daughters?" I asked.

"Yes, my daddy is a General or something or other in England" she replied.

"Do you like my tits?" she asked.

"Yes, there very nice" I replied,

"Well, what are you waiting for, come and feel at them" she said.

"Don't be silly, you're an officer's daughter" I said.

"What's that got to do with anything, I'm still a girl, well if you don't feel then I'll go around the camp until I find someone who will" she said, sounding a little disappointed.

"No don't do that, stay here" I said.

"I want a good time, so come on, you know how to fuck don't you?" she asked.

The word fuck just didn't seem right when she said it.

What was I thinking of, any other girl and I would have been into her like a rat up a drain pipe.

"Come on, up you get" I said, pulling her up by her arms onto her feet, I held her against me to stop her from falling, for a moment I could feel her breasts pressing against my chest, I lifted her dress straps back onto shoulders.

"Let's go and sit in here" I said, leading her back into the front office.

"Meany" she complained, "Don't you like me?"

"Like you, I think you're very beautiful" I said, sitting her down in the office chair.

"Don't you like my tits?" she asked again.

"Yes, I think your tits are very beautiful too" I replied.

"So why don't you want to fuck me?" she asked.

"Because you've had too much to drink and you don't know what you're doing" I explained.

"I'll make us some coffee" I said.

"Play with me then, spoilsport, make me cum" she said rubbing herself between the legs.

I knelt down beside the chair, cupping her breasts in my hands, caressing and nipping her nipples that hardened to my touch. She slumped down in the chair resting her feet on the table she opened her legs while I removed her panties and pushed my fingers into her cunt and finger fucked her. She was wet and I could smell her, bending forward I kissed her breasts, working my way down her body towards the small mound between her legs.

"More" she moaned and then crossed her legs, clamping my hand between her thighs and my fingers inside her.

"Are you happy now?" I asked.

"Yes that was great. Thank you. But what about you?" she asked looking at the bulge in the front of my trousers.

"Don't worry about me" I replied. Actually thinking to myself 'Guess who's off for a wank when you've gone lady.'

"Come here" she said unbuckling my belt, unzipping me and removing my cock from my pants she started to wank me.

"Cum on my tits and belly" she said wanking me faster.

"I'm cumming" I shouted, my load shooting all over her from crotch to face.

"Fantastic" she screamed. "Bloody fantastic, but one day you're going to fuck me properly."

"You'd better go and get cleaned up in there" I said pointing towards the back room.

I made us both a coffee and we sat talking.

She was on summer holidays from some boarding school in England and was staying with her aunt and uncle, a Captain in the regiment.

She was now starting to sober up a little and went on to explain that she had been invited to the ball by her uncle providing she did not drink any alcohol.

'No alcohol. That worked a treat' I thought.

She then explained that a spotty face young 2nd Lieutenant had tried to get her into his room in the mess.

We only had one 2nd Lieutenant on camp, a useless little twat, all brains and no common sense, so I knew who she meant.

"Why didn't you go with him?" I asked

"His hands where all over me and I didn't like him, so I escaped and came up here out of the way" she replied.

She was sobering up quicker now every time one of her shoulder straps slipped she caught it and replaced it back on her shoulder, so she was definitely more aware of what she was doing.

"Mercedes" a voice shouted from outside.

"Mercedes, is that you" I asked.

"Yes" she replied.

"Nice name, what's your surname Benz?" I asked smiling, but she didn't get the joke.

"Mercedes" someone shouted again.

"You'd better go" I said.

"I will but before I do, will you do me just one more little favour?" she asked.

"What's that?" I asked.

"Kiss me" she said.

I leaned over put my arms around her and kissed her on the lips.

"Now go and behave yourself" I said.

"Thank you" she said getting out of her chair.

"Bye" I said.

"Bye" she said, closing the door behind her.

"Bye" I said again, and watched her through the window as she skipped down the steps to be met at the bottom by Captain Red,

'Oh! No, Captain Red', 'Was he her uncle' I thought.

Then I realised he had seen her leave the radio room and who was in the radio room, me.

'Oh! God, I'm in the shit', I thought.

Too late now I'll just have to wait and see what happens?

'I hope she doesn't say I did anything wrong or I could be on a rape charge for nothing.

I decided to stay in the radio room for the rest of the night just in case Red came looking for me, I didn't want him to find me in the barrack room and start asking questions in front of the other lads.

Sat in the chair with my feet up on the desk I was nodding off to sleep when as expected Red walked in.

'Fuck me I'm for it now' I thought

I jumped up and stood to attention.

"Sit down Sarge, I want a word with you" he said.

'Sarge, he called me Sarge, instead of my full surname'.

"Can you explain to me why my niece was in here with you earlier?" he asked.

"I haven't touched her Sir, we were just talking" I stammered, sounding as guilty as hell.

"Calm down and explain to me everything that was said and everything that happened" he said.

I regained my composure.

'He's remarkably calm himself' I thought.

I knew I hadn't done anything wrong, but what had she told him and with that I recanted the whole story from when she walked in drunk to when she left, of course I left out the part where she had asked me to have sex, and I didn't mention her being half naked, but I did make a point of telling him about what she had said about the young Lieutenant.

"Thank you, Sarge, that's exactly what my niece has just told me" he said.

"And you believe her?" I asked, still sounding as guilty as hell.

"If I didn't, you wouldn't still be sitting there, you'd be in the guard room on a charge" he said.

"Thank you sir, you are a Gent" I said.

"No. Thank you, Sarge, you're the gentleman, if it hadn't been for you I dread to think of what might have happened to her, someone could easily have raped her" he said.

"We're not all uncouth morons, Sir" I commented.

"Indeed Sarge, it would appear to be so" he replied.

'I wish he would stop calling me 'Sarge' it's unsettling when an officer calls you by your nickname'.

"What are you doing in here?" he asked

"I come up here to clear my head and think, sometimes I prefer to on my own" I said.

"Oh! I'm sorry I'm not disturbing you now, am I?" he said all apologetic.

I didn't answer because I wasn't sure what to say, he seemed to have forgotten that he was the officer and I was the private, we continued our conversation as if we had been friends for years.

"Who's that talking?" he asked.

I had an old radio switched on with the sound turned down.

"Oh, that, it's an old A13 ground to air radio, I've managed to get it working, it picks up all sorts of rubbish" I said, pointing to the corner.

"Their speaking Chinese" he said.

"Yes, Sir" I said.

"And you understand them?" he asked.

"Yes, Sir, well some of it" I replied.

"You speak Chinese?" he asked.

"Yes, Sir, my girlfriend taught me" I replied.

"Yes, I heard you had a Chinese girlfriend what is she like?" he asked.

"Twenty years old, good looking, intelligent, nice, the same has any other girl I suppose, except she's got slanty eyes" I said, trying to make a joke.

Well, yes, she will have if she's Chinese" he smiled, glancing back at the radio.

"Who is it and what are they saying?" he asked.

"It's the red army over the border in China, just general chit chat, who's going where, who's arriving and radio checks, that's all" I said.

He stood up and walked over to the radio and turned the tuner.

"That's fast", he said, listening to some Morse code.

"About twenty words a minute" I said, picking up a pencil and writing the last part down.

Ten degrees north weather warning strong winds south westerly with heavy showers Alpha Romeo...

"Just a weather forecast, Sir" I said, passing him the bit of paper I had scribbled the message on.

"You read it at that speed?" he asked, excitedly.

"Yes, Sir" I replied, wondering why he sounded so surprised.

"I've been reading your personal army record, don't worry I read every one's, I see that you had a private education and then went on to Art College, with good grades in most major subjects, and you also hold a full driving licence.

Why didn't you join the transport platoon, and have you ever thought about becoming an officer? I can get you the application forms for Sandhurst" he said.

"Excuse my next remark, Sir, It's is not meant to be offensive, but I don't speak posh enough to be an officer" I said, ignoring the question about transport.

"You sound, as you put it. Posh to me" he said.

It was then I realised that I had dropped my Yorkshire accent and I was speaking the way I used to when I was a child growing up.

Thank you, but no thank you, Sir I don't want to be an officer" I replied.

"Well what would you say to becoming an NCO?" he asked.

"No thanks again, Sir, I don't really want to be an NCO either" I said.

"Why on earth not, with your qualifications you should easily pass and think of the extra money" he said.

"I don't need the money, Sir" I said, without thinking.

"No, you probably have more money than I do, you come from quite a wealthy family don't you, what exactly is it your father does?" he asked.

I didn't answer and he didn't ask again, he must have realised it was none of his business what my financial circumstances were.

I didn't want anyone to know, especially the lads, not because they might want to borrow from me or even want me to pay for everything, I just didn't want them to know about that part of my life, I wanted to be one of the lads and I didn't think I would fit in if they knew.

'I wish he would fuck off and leave me alone' I thought, he was becoming a pain in the arse with all his stupid questions he already knew more about me than I felt comfortable with.

I was really getting pissed off with him now.

"Sir, if you don't mind..." I was cut short by someone opening the door.

"Are you coming back to the ball uncle?" asked Mercedes, looking at me and blushing slightly. I wasn't sure if she was embarrassed because she had wanted sex with me or disappointed because I turned her down.

"Hello again" she said.

"Are you feeling better now?" I asked her.

She didn't answer, perhaps because Red was present.

"Come on then uncle, we're waiting for you" she said.

"Be a good girl and answer the lad he asked you if you were feeling better now" he said.

"Oh, yes, much better thank you" she said.

"You're welcome" I said.

"Sir, please don't let the lads know anything about this or what's in my record file" I said.

"Don't worry your secrets are safe" he said, putting his arm around Mercedes shoulder and walking out of the door with her.

"Bye" shouted Mercedes, descending the steps.

"Bye" I said, but I don't think she heard me.

Thank god he's gone.

Now remind me again, why I'm in the army.

Oh! Yes, I won a bet didn't I?

No not really, I wasn't sure what I wanted to do with my life, the army just seemed to be a convenient place to park up for a few years, and it was never meant to be a career.

"What's wrong?" asked Justin.

"Nothing" I replied.

"Jeanie says you haven't been to see her for a couple of weeks now and she doesn't know why, she seemed a bit upset" he said.

"No reason, I just needed a break from her" I replied.

"She getting you down?" he asked.

It had been two weeks since I last saw her.

"I'll go and phone her" I said, and with that I went to the phone box at the end of our block.

"Hello" said a voice on the other end.

"Can I speak to Jeanie please?" I asked.

"Hi Sarge, it Lily, Jeanie not in at moment" she said.

"Ok, tell her I will see her tonight at six" I said.

"She not be long, you come now" said Lily.

"I'm on my way, tell her to wait for me" I said.

"Ok, bye" said Lily and hung up.

I went back to the barrack room, got ready to go out and caught the bus to Shaukiwan.

I had started buying her little gifts so I decide to go into a jewellery shop and buy her something nice as a peace offering so to speak, I decided against a ring, I did buy her one once, but she refused to take it from me, she thought I wanted to marry her, so I settled on a gold and diamond necklace, I was on my own, so none of the lads knew what I was doing, if they didn't know about it, it meant that they couldn't take the piss.

I arrived at the flat on entering I shouted.
"Hello, anyone home."
There was no answer, 'Where is everyone' I thought.
"One minute" shouted Lily from the bathroom.
I put the necklace in Jeanie's room under her pillow so no one would see it and went to sit in the lounge, where was Jeanie, Lily said she wouldn't be long.
I could hear the water running in the bathroom.
"Where is everyone?" I shouted to Lily.
"What? I no hear you" she shouted back.
"Where is everyone?" I shouted again.
"Come here, I no hear you" she shouted.
I opened the bathroom door and put my head around it.
"Where is? Err! Fuck me" I blurted out when I saw Lily bending over cleaning the bath completely naked.
I was getting an erection just looking at her.
Oh! I'm sorry" I said.
"You come in, it OK" she said.
"OK, what?" I said closing the door behind me.
"OK, you want fuck me?" She said, still bending over the bath and waggling her bum towards me.
Had she tricked me into coming to the flat early so I would be on my own with her?
"Is this, one day, Lily?" I asked.
"It one day" she replied.
I walked over to her as she started to stand up straight.
"No stay there" I said running my hands up her back and around to the front of her body cupping her breasts, then running them down her stomach and between her legs as I leaned over her.
"Listen" I said. "We do not tell Jeanie or Frank or any of the others about this, it's our secret".
"OK, I no tell" she said.
I moved one hand from her front and placed it between her legs from behind; she opened her legs and held onto the edge of the bath with her hands as I rubbed her. She didn't make a sound, has she rocked gently backwards and forwards on my hand letting my fingers slide into her, until she tensed up and trapped my hand between her thighs.
"You fuck me now please" she said.
"Let me go and get a condom" I said.
"No, you no need one" she said.
"Why, you don't want to get pregnant do you?" I asked.

"I not have baby, I take pill" she said.

I felt her shudder and have another orgasm.

"Hurry, fuck me now" she said.

"Why? Are you on the pill, Jeanie and Monica aren't, they use condoms", I asked.

"They on pill also, you fucked them both in bath without condom, didn't you? But they make you use condom so you not too sensitive and cum too soon, now please fuck me" she pleaded.

I had undone my trousers and was ready to take her.

"Please" she said, pushing her bum against me.

I slipped into her from behind has she had another orgasm, pushing herself further onto me.

"Oh! That nice, now fuck" she demanded.

I held her each side with her hips and pushed into her.

I was fucking Lily; this is what I had been waiting for. Unlike Jeanie or Monica, Lily made no noise at all, I knew when she was having an orgasm because I could feel her tense up has she tightened around me.

"Now" she said, almost in a whisper, "Now."

I moved faster and let myself cum into her has she tightened on me again.

I hope she was telling the truth about the pill.

"You no need condom, you no cum too soon, you waited for me" she said.

I stayed inside her until my erection went down.

"You go my room now, get in bed and wait" she said.

"Where are Jeanie and the others?" I asked.

"They no home for long time yet, Tammy working, Monica at college, Jeanie visit mother in Kowloon", she explained, counting them off on her fingers has she named each one.

I did as I was asked and went to her bedroom and got into bed, it smelt clean and fresh, reminding me of home. It had been many years since I was last at home to stay, more often than not I would visit and leave again the same day, even when I had leave I very rarely stayed at home, preferring to book into an hotel or shack up with some girl I knew from my college days, but their numbers were getting few and far between has they found themselves husbands and settled down. I had almost forgotten what it was like.

Lily entered the room, she didn't speak, just climbed into bed, straddled me and lay down on top of me, I very soon got another erection, she felt this and moved herself so that I slid inside her, we laid for a long time in each other's arms, not speaking or moving, just very still, very quiet, just holding each other, every so often she would tense up, has I felt her orgasm, then she lay very still again, until the next one.

'I wasn't even moving inside this girl and she was cuming every couple of minutes', I thought.

I tried to thrust upwards into her, but she stopped me, she was in control, I wasn't moving, I didn't need to, she was using her muscles to squeeze me inside her. It felt great; a girl had never done this to me before.

Then without any warning, she sat bolt upright on me and rode me like a bucking bronco, collapsing back onto me as we both came.

We lay very still; my erection was not going down as I felt her once again squeezing me inside her. Then once more without warning she sat up and did the same thing again.

'If this is what she did with Frank, then he must have remarkable self control, no wonder they were quiet', I thought.

We lay quiet again; as my erection went down I slipped out of her and she rolled off me and lay by my side.

"Thank you" she said, in Chinese.

"Thank you for what, I should be the one thanking you" I said, kissing her.

"No, thank you for letting me do it my way" she said.

"Well, you let me do it my way in the bathroom" I said.

"We had better get up now, look at the time" she said.

"Remember don't tell anyone" I reminded her.

"OK, our secret" she replied, getting out of bed.

I went to the bathroom to wash and clean up; I didn't want Jeanie to smell Lily on me later.

On my return to the lounge Lily was sat in the armchair, I sat on the sofa, she was now very talkative and we sat chatting, we didn't speak about what we had just done. It was as if the last few hours had never taken place.

The door opened and Jeanie walked in.

"Hi, I'm home" she shouted.

"Hi" shouted Lily,

"Bugger off we don't want any" I shouted, in a made up voice, hoping she wouldn't realise it was me.

"Who's that?" she asked.

"I don't know" I replied in my own voice.

She came running up the passage and flung herself on top of me on the sofa.

"You bugger off, you bugger, where, have you been?" she asked, trying to kiss my face off.

I was tempted to say, next door shagging the arse off Lily, but I didn't.

"Working" I replied.

"How long you been here?" she asked, reverting back to English.

"Not long about ten minutes".

The door opened again, this time it was Tammy, Justin and Monica.

"Hey up Sarge, thought you might be here" said Justin.

"How long you been here?" asked Monica.

"About ten minutes" I said, again.

"Ten minutes, you liar, you left the barrack room hours ago" said Justin.

"Bet you been here hours" said Monica.

"No I haven't" I said.

"You have, you been here hours, you been jig a jig with Lily", laughed Monica.

"No, we not jig a jig", said Lily.

Lily looked over at me as if to say, 'we are going to get caught out'.

"No I haven't, I went shopping" I replied, remembering the necklace under Jeanie's pillow.

"What you buy?" asked Jeanie.

"Go and look in your room" I said.

She ran off into her room like a little child at Christmas.

"I no find anything", she said, putting her head back around the door.

"Keep looking" I said, "Under your pillow".

There was a squeal of delight when she found the necklace, and came skipping back down the passage towards me, throwing her arms around my neck she kissed me.

"Thank you, it beautiful" she said, holding the necklace up for me to put around her neck.

The other girls gathered around her, discussing if it was real and how much it was worth.

"You get fuckin dafter, buying her things" said Justin.

"I didn't buy it, I found it in the street" I said, joking.

"You find in street, we give to police" said Jeanie, trying to take it off.

"No, I'm joking" I said, stopping her.

"I bought it, I didn't find it" I said.

"You sure, you no find it, you show me receipt or I no believe you" she said.

'Oh! Shit, how can I do that without her or the others seeing the price I paid.

What a stupid joke, I should have known it would back fire on me' I thought.

"Just a moment" I said, pulling the receipt from my pocket and trying to let her read it, while I held it with my thumb over the price.

"OK, I believe you" said Jeanie, just then Monica jumped up and grabbed it out of my hand.

"Wow, it real, it gold and diamonds, pay plenty" she said.

"Monica, please don't say" I begged her.

"How much?" asked Tammy.

"I tell you later" replied Monica, handing the receipt out for me to take, but this time Justin grabbed it.

"For god's sake, give me the receipt and pack it in, it's none of your business how much I paid" I said.

"One thousand seven hundred and ninety five dollars, you crazy bastard" said Justin, very slowly.

"Ah, for fucks sake Justin, why did you do that? I asked.

"How much?" asked Tammy.

He repeated the figures again, just to make sure he hadn't read it wrong.

"Where the fuck, you get that kind of money from?" asked Justin.

"He been saving up" laughed Lily.

"He's done more than saved up, that's more than one month's wages" said Justin.

"He rob a bank" said Tammy.

"Shut the fuck up" I said, by now I had lost my temper with them all, including Jeanie and she hadn't done anything wrong.

"I no want it, it too much money" said Jeanie, trying to take it off again.

"No, leave it on" I demanded.

"No too much money, it make me look like you pay me for jig a jig and I not prostitute" she said.

"If you take it off I will go out of that door and you will never see me again, it was a gift to a friend not payment to a prostitute" I shouted at her.

"I'm your friend but you don't buy me gifts like that" said Justin, taking the piss in his camp voice.

"And you can fuck off as well" I said to him.

"And what about all the other things I've bought you, how much do you think they cost, did I give them to a friend or were they payment for your services" I shouted at Jeanie.

By the time I stopped shouting Jeanie had removed the necklace and was stood there with it in her hand.

I looked at her, looked at the necklace then looked at the others, what was I waiting for, none of them spoke another word, had Jeanie really intended to remove the necklace, if so, why?, didn't she understand it was a gift, didn't she understand that I was in love with her, I wasn't getting any reaction from any of them, I shrugged my shoulders and walked to the door, just as I opened it Frank walked in.

"What's all the noise about? I can hear you lot on the stairs" he asked.

"Ask them" I said, and left.

Before the door closed, I heard him asking what was wrong with me.

As I left the building I could hear Jeanie at the top of the stairs crying and shouting me back, but I kept on walking away.

'Fuck you' I thought to myself, 'Oh, I already have done and paid you for the pleasure'.

I decided to walk to Wan Chai and get pissed in one of the bars.

I must have walked about half a mile when I heard Justin shout me. I looked back and he was about fifty yard behind me, I slowed down while he caught up.

"What the fuck do you want?" I asked.

"Look, we're sorry, we were out of order, come back

Jeanie is upset and crying" he said.

"Let the ungrateful sod cry, I don't give a fuck anymore" I said.

"Calm down and lets go for a drink" he said.

"Fuck off and get back to your boy bitch" I said, pushing him away.

He stopped walking and looked at me in disbelief.

Oh! Christ what had I said.

"I'm sorry Justin, I really am, I didn't mean to say that, you have your secrets and I have mine" I said.

"It may help if you shared your secret" he said.

"Mates" I said and held my hand out.

"Mates" he replied and shook my hand.

"What do you want to do, go back to the flat or go for a drink?" he asked.

"Drink" I said.

"Where we going then, The Mermaid?" he asked.

"We're not really dressed for what I have in mind, but if you want to know my secret you will have to come with me" I said.

I flagged down a taxi and we jumped in.

"Queens Road Central please driver" I said.

"What the hell we going there for?" asked Justin.

"You'll see" I said.

I leaned forward and whispered to the driver,

"The Hilton please"

"Yes Sir" he replied.

The cab pulled into the entrance of the hotel and the concierge opened the door touch his cap and welcomed us.

"Good evening Mr Sargeant, welcome back" he said.

"What the fuck are we doing here?" asked Justin.

"And what's with the "Mr Sargeant welcome back stuff?""

"Shut up and follow me" I said.

We walked into the lobby and up to the desk.

"Are there any messages for me?" I asked the desk clerk.

"Just the one Sir" he said, handing me an envelope.

It was a letter from my mother.

"Come on" I said to Justin but he just stood there gawping.

In my suite on the twentieth floor, Justin bounced on the bed.

"Don't go trashing the place and don't sling the TV out the window, we're not pop stars" I said.

"No but you live like one, so come on spill the beans, what are you doing in here?" he asked, follow by a string of questions, who, where, why and what for.

I just about gave him my complete life story.

"So what are you doing in the army?" he asked.

"Slumming, seeing how the other half live, oh I don't know" I replied.

"If I were you, I know where I would be" he said.

"Go on then, where?" I asked.

"On some exotic beach or a yacht somewhere surrounded by beautiful girls" he said.

"Girls" I said, laughing.

"Well, some boys as well then" he laughed.

"Been there, done that" I said.

"What, with boys?" he asked.

"You know what I mean" I said.

"So come on then, what are you worth? That's if you want to tell me", he asked.

"Not sure, probably somewhere around two million" I replied.

"Fuck me, you rich bastard, do the powers that be know?"he asked, meaning the army.

"They know I come from a wealth family, but I think, that they think, I just get an allowance from my parents.

"Where you get it all from?" he asked.

"Most of it has built up in trust funds set up for me by my grandparents, plus some investments, plus some from my parents and some left to me in wills, and when I reached the age of twenty one, I took control of it" I explained.

"So you were a millionaire before you joined up" he said.

"No stupid, I've only just gone twenty one, haven't I" I said.

"When?" he asked

"A few weeks ago" I replied.

"You never said, and if we had known we could have had a piss up for you" he said.

"No wonder I kept my mouth shut, the thought of you lot singing happy birthday to me was enough to make anyone keep quiet, and anyway it's too late now" I said.

"Are you going to tell the other lads and the girls your rich?" he asked.

"What do you think? I suppose I might have to now, because you won't be able to keep your mouth shut for two minutes" I said, it was not meant to be a question, more of a sarcastic remark.

"I'll not say anything" he answered.

"Yer like you didn't tell everyone the price of the necklace" I said.

"Look, I'm sorry, I only meant it as a joke" he said.

"OK, forget it, let's not start that again and no I'm not going to tell them, well not yet anyway, also I don't want the army to find out or they will discharge me, so you keep it shut" I said.

"I'll keep your secret from the powers that be, if you keep mine and Tammy's about me being gay, I don't want kicking out of the army either", he said, this was the first time I had heard him actually admit he was gay.

"Deal" I replied.

"You want to go back to the flat now?" he asked.

"Not sure if I ever want to go back there again, let's find somewhere else to go" I said.

"Come on lets go back to the flat, Jeanie's a great girl, she'll miss you if you pack in with her after all this time, and I know you'll miss her too" he said.

He was right I was missing her already, even if she was not the type of girl you could take home to mother.

Come on, let's be realistic, what type of girl lets you sleep with her cousin then wants you to sleep with her friend, certainly not the type that would make a good wife and mother, there would be no trust between us, and as she had said 'it only fun', would it stay 'only fun', if see knew the truth about me or would she become a gold digger and want to marry me just for the money, there was one way to find out and that was to tell her and see what her reaction is.

I think I may have just fallen out of love with Jeanie, so if I go back to her it will be on my terms, for the sex only and what I can get out of it.

"Are we going back to the flat now" asked Justin.

I could see he was inpatient to get back there so reluctantly I agreed.

Before we arrived at the flat, we had arranged that Justin should go in first and tell Jeanie that I was not coming back, just to see what her reaction was.

"Hi" Justin shouted entering the flat.

"Where Sarge?" asked Tammy.

"He says, he's not coming back and doesn't want to see Jeanie anymore" he replied.

Jeanie heard him with tears filling her eyes she screamed and ran into her room slammed the door behind her.

Monica was about to follow her, when I entered the flat and stopped her, putting a finger across my lips, I moved her away from the door, she smiled and kissed me on the cheek.

"Shush, quiet" I said, I could hear Jeanie sobbing, I opened the door, she was laid with her back to me, her head buried in the pillow and wearing the necklace, this was not the reaction I had expected, I lay on the bed next to her, and put my arm around her.

"He no love me anymore, I been stupid, stupid girl" she sobbed; she must have thought I was one of the girls.

"Forget about him then" I said.

"Sarge!" she screamed, turning over to face me.

"You come back, you no leave me, I sorry" she said,

We didn't leave the bedroom all night.

Out of the blue, and for what seem no reason, me and Justin were summoned to see the CO, we knew we hadn't done anything wrong, the only thing we could think of was, were our secrets out.

We were marched into his office by Raggy Tash and stood to attention in front of the C.O's desk.

"Right Private Sidebottom how long have you been at war with Vietnam?" asked the CO.

"I'm not a war with Vietnam, Sir" replied Justin, looking puzzled.

"OK, I'll ask you the same question Private Sargeant" said the CO.

"I'm not at war with Vietnam either Sir, the Americans are" I said, wondering what the hell he was talking about, could it be when we were insulting the American sailors in the Mermaid Bar, no that can't be it, that was me and Frank, Justin wasn't with us, and anyway he said Vietnam not America.

"Do you remember working in the stores packing the old equipment away" he said.

"Yes Sir" we both replied.

"How did you mark the boxes?" he asked.

"With U.S, like always" answered Justin.

"Exactly, you marked them U.S. and not U stroke S" he said.

"We didn't, did we, sorry sir" I said, and to be honest I couldn't remember how we had marked them.

"What's wrong with that, Sir?" asked Justin.

"What's wrong with it, I will tell you what's wrong with it, somewhere along the line because of your incompetence the boxes were sent to Vietnam by the Americans, who thought they were supplies for their troops in the field.

"But sir......." said Justin, trying to but in.

"No buts Sidebottom, the best is yet to come, the American Air Force dropped the boxes by parachute to re supply their troops but someone got the wrong co-ordinates and they ended up bombing the Vietcong with our useless equipment" he said, trying to keep a straight face.

'This has got to be a wind up' I thought.

"But sir, that's got nothing to do with us, we may have labelled the boxes wrong but we didn't ship them to Vietnam, we didn't get the co-ordinates wrong, and we didn't bomb the Vietcong" said Justin, protesting.

"Surely the Americans would check equipment before sending it anywhere, especially something as important as troops in the field, Sir" I said, still convinced this was a wind up and trying to catch him out.

"You would think so" said the C.O, as he burst out laughing.

"Oh! It's a joke" said Justin.

"Not quite, the equipment has to be paid for" said the C.O.

"So it's true and not a wind up, Sir" I said.

"Oh, yes it's true, I'm afraid, the Vietcong are running around with our radios, so if you hear any Vietnamese on that A13 of yours in the radio room, you know who to blame" he replied.

"Yep, the Americans" I said.

"I'm sorry lads, I know it's not entirely your fault and it's the funniest thing I've heard in a long time but this has come from the top brass and will have go on your record,

I have been ordered to stop you both ten pound a week out of your pay until further notice, think yourself lucky and don't complain some of them wanted you both on a charge and jailed, it is only because your Platoon Sergeant and myself put in a good word for you that got you off so lightly" said the C.O.

"Got off lightly, I don't call ten pounds a week getting off lightly, it's the Americans who should be paying for it not us" said Justin.

"Shut up and accept it" I whispered to Justin.

"Thank you, Sir" said Justin.

"Thank you, Sir" I said, and with that Raggy Tash marched us out of the office.

"Ten fuckin quid a week" moaned Justin.

"You heard him, it could have been worse" I said.

"Yer, but ten fuckin quid" whined Justin again.

"Ah, stop moaning, we've got it to pay and going on about it won't make it any better" I said.

"It's OK for you, ten quid is nowt to you" he said.

"It's not the money that's worrying me, it's the thought of what is written on my record" I said.

"Yer", laughed Justin, moving his hands from side to side as if to indicate writing an entry in a book.

"Private Sargeant would have made an excellent soldier if he hadn't been responsible for bombing North Vietnam while serving with the military in Hong Kong, six out of ten, good effort, but must try harder" he said.

"Hey, we must be the only two British soldiers in the world to have ever been responsible for bombing Vietnam, when we have never been near the place." I said.

"Beep, beep, beep, beep, Urgent News Flash, Leader of the North Vietnamese Republic Ho Chi Minh was today brained by old British radio and other junk in Ha Noi City, beep, beep" said Justin, making a noise like a teleprinter.

After that everyone was told never to mark anything with the letters U or S, just in case the Americans thought it was theirs.

Justin and I were probably right in the first place. U.S. = useless.

Coming up to Christmas 1969, someone had the bright idea to turn one of the lecture rooms into a bar so we could have a platoon party, a stage and bar were built the place was decorated with cam nets and coloured lighting, and looked fairly good when it was finished.

Booze was bought, a Chinese bar man was hired and some of the lads in the band who had formed a pop group agreed to play for the night.

The theme was supposed to be a hippy night, so it was bell bottoms, flowered shirts, beads, and because we all had short hair so wigs were donned and we looked a right set of prats.

The married men came with their wives and teenage daughters, they were the you can look type of daughter, but you're a dead man if you touch, the only problem was, we were about thirty girls short of a party.

The lads who were organising it were discussing what kind of party it was going to be without girls when my name got mentioned.

I didn't even plan on being there so why should I care.

I could get pissed with these lads anytime I wanted, we didn't need a party to do that, and I definitely wasn't going to dance with any of them, so what was the point.

"Hey! Sarge, you've got a Chinese girl friend are you bringing her to the party?" asked one of them.

"Probably" I said, not wanting at this point to let them know that I may not be there myself.

"Can you bring thirty of her friends?" he asked.

"Where the fuck do you supposed to get thirty girls from?" I asked.

"Raid a girl's school" said another lad.

'Girls school, college, that's not as daft as it sounds, I wonder if Jeanie's got thirty college friends that want to go to a party' I thought.

"And if I get some girls, how do you propose I get them here?" I asked.

"Taxi" he said.

"Yer right, thirty girls, four girls to a taxi, that's eight taxi's here and eight taxi's back, it will cost you a fortune" I said.

"I think I can help you there" said Captain Red who was stood behind us listening to our conversation.

"How, Sir?" I asked.

"I will get the duty driver to pick them up and take them home afterwards in the regimental bus" he said.

The regimental bus was a beat up old green thing used by the band to go to and from concerts.

"That would be great, Sir" said one of the lads.

"OK then Sarge, see that girlfriend of yours, get things organised and let me have the details" said Capt Red.

There he goes again, calling me by my nickname.

I was given some invitations to hand out to the girls who were coming, I just passed them onto Jeanie and let her get on with it.

Eventually she manages to get twenty eight girls to agree to come, how she did it, god knows.

The details were passed onto Red who in turn passed them onto the duty driver.

He seem pleased with the idea that he would have twenty eight girls on his bus and bragged around the camp what he was going to do with this one and what he was going to do to that one, he should be so lucky, then again if any of them were like Jeanie or Monica, or Lily if it comes that, then he had it made, he would get a least one of them.

Justin, Frank, Billy, myself and the girls made our own arrangements to get there.

On the night of the party, we were sat in the makeshift bar with our girls, Jeanie, Monica, Lily and Tammy, waiting for the bus to arrive the other lads flocked around the girls like flies around a shit pot.

While being chatted up by the lads, the girls were talking to each other in Chinese and giggling.

"Look at him, he looks like a good fuck" said Monica.

"Yes, and look at the cute bum on that one" said Lily.

"He's OK too" commented Jeanie.

"Go on then" I said to her.

"No, I'm only joking, I stay with you" she said, in a mixture of Chinese and English.

Monica and Lily were still discussing the merits of the other lads when the bus pulled up outside.

"Will you two behave yourself", I said.

The girls piled out of the bus, all except one or two were wearing very short miniskirts, I've never seen so many legs in one place at one time in all my life, wow!, nice legs, what time do they open.

Most of the lads rushed outside to meet the girls. Meet could be the wrong word, it was more akin to grab a girl quick before the supply runs out, only the shy ones missed out.

The bus pulled away and I noticed that one of the girls had stayed on the bus with the driver, so he did get lucky after all. The bus driver didn't drive back down the hill to the transport yard where he should have parked up, but straight up the hill to the top of the camp, he stopped and switched off all the lights. He would have to go some if he were going to make that rock on its springs, the bus, I mean, not the girl.

The party went without a hitch, the booze flowed, the band played, everyone danced and most of the girls got the arses shagged off them by the randy bastards in our platoon, one girl was even seen under a table giving one of our Corporals a blow job, while his wife danced with someone else.

The lads who were unlucky and didn't get a girl off the bus were trying to chat the married men's wives and daughters up, but none of them were having any success,

The party was drawing to a close and the room was almost empty, with most of the lads outside getting their end away.

"You taking Jeanie home or what?" asked Justin.

"Or what" I said.

"Up the hill", he said, meaning the radio room.

"Yep, up the hill, I'm feeling too pissed to go all the way back to the flat" I replied.

"What, up the hill?" asked Jeanie.

"Up the hill, I'll show you soon" I said.

"We're going back to the flat with the girls, see you later" said Justin.

The bus stopped outside to collect the girls and take them home, but only about fifteen boarded it, the driver said he couldn't wait any longer, so he drove off, that meant that somewhere on camp there were still about thirteen missing girls, awhile later the guard was dispatched to go and find them, one was found behind the NAAFI, fast asleep with her knickers around her ankles, someone said later that the guard who found her, also gave her a good seeing to before escorting her to the guard room to wait for transport home, one was found in the swimming pool completely naked and she didn't know where her clothes were, I also heard that the guard who found her, stripped off and joined her in the pool, they were then found by another guard who also stripped off and joined in, one of them left a used condom floating in the water, another girl was found in the officers mess, probably that randy little Second Lieutenant, was responsible for that one, some were found in bed with lads who weren't even at the party, and some girls were found just roaming around the camp in a drunken state, and in various stages of undress, going from one barrack room to the next, being gang banged senseless by everyone and anyone who happened to find them.

I wonder how many fair haired, blue eyed babies were born in Shaukiwan nine month later.

On the way up to the radio room with Jeanie we found one of the missing girls, she was the one I had seen stay on the bus with the driver.

When we told her she had missed the bus, she started to cry, Jeanie tried to calm her down. We couldn't stay where we were for fear of getting caught by the guard, so I hurried them both into the radio room.

"Keep quiet and don't put the lights on" I said, locking the door behind us.

"Will you take me home?", she asked Jeanie in Chinese.

"I'm not going home I'm staying here with my boyfriend" said Jeanie.

"How will I get home?" she asked.

"I'll send for a taxi" I said.

"No, she can stay here with us, can't she?" asked Jeanie.

"Not if she doesn't want to, we can't force her" I replied,

"Anyway what happened with the bus driver and why was she on her own?" I asked.

Jeanie took her into the backroom and spoke to her in a whisper, making it hard for me to hear, but I did manage to catch some of it, apparently the bus driver wanted oral sex, so she got off the bus.

They called me into the backroom.

"She going to stay" said Jeanie, in English.

"What's her name?" I asked.

"My name is Lin" said the girl, smiling.

She was a pretty little thing, probably about eighteen years old, Eurasian, with a round face, short light brown hair, blue eyes and spoke better English than I did.

"Do you really want to stay or is Jeanie making you stay?" I asked her.

"I really want to stay, that's if you don't mind" she replied.

"I don't mind but we are going to bed" I said.

"Jig a jig" she said, looking at Jeanie.

She spoke to Jeanie in Chinese and to me in English, not knowing that I understood both.

Jeanie just nodded her head.

"OK, I will sleep in the chair in here" she said returning to the front office.

God knows how I was going to get two girls out of camp in the next day, I hadn't worked out that part of my plan.

She settled down in the front office and I went to bed with Jeanie.

"How well do you know her?" I asked Jeanie.

"She just goes to the same college as me" she replied.

"So not really all that well then" I said.

"She is OK, don't worry, she won't say anything" she said.

The old army bed was squeaking, as they always do, so I knew Lin could hear everything that we were doing, and I felt very uncomfortable, this just wasn't working out like I wanted.

'Oh! To hell with it' I thought, and we both fell asleep.

I was woken up by Jeanie touching me.

"Don't, Jeanie, let me sleep" I said.

I didn't move or open my eyes, I felt her climbed on top of me, please get off me and let me sleep" I said.

Then she just leaned forward and kissed me on the lips.

'That's not Jeanie', I thought, opening my eyes to find Lin sat on me, had I just had sex with Lin, I was trying to get my brain in gear, yes I must have.

"Where's Jeanie?" I asked.

"Here" said Jeanie, who was knelt at the side of the bed.

"You've done it again, haven't you" I said.

"You like?" she asked.

"It's a bit too late to ask now, isn't it" I replied.

"You no mind" said, Jeanie.

Lin never spoke she just sat there looking down at me.

"Come on you" I said, getting more comfortable under her.

"We've started so let's finish" I said.

I made love to both girls for the rest of the night.

Sat with Rod in the NAAFI later the next day, one lad from 'B' Company was overheard saying, he had been on area cleaning duty picking rubbish up at the back of the lecture rooms and had never seen so many used condoms, then he talked about how the guards were finding girls all over camp last night.

"Did they find them all?" I asked, knowing they hadn't found Jeanie or Lin.

"They found the one I was with" said Rod.

"Where were you?" I asked.

"In my bed, just coming up to the vinegar stroke when this Corporal pulls me off her and takes her to the guardroom" he said.

"You poor bastard", I said.

"Don't matter though, I had a wank on her knickers instead" he said.

"You've cum on her kegs" I said.

"Yep what else could I do, she had gone" he said, pulling the knickers out of his pocket and putting them over his head.

"Hummm! Smell that pussy" he said inhaling deeply.

"Fuck off, yer dirty bastard" I said.

"You only got one pair", said a lad, looking over Rod's shoulder.

"Look at these, three pairs, I fucked three of them, last night I did, look at them", he bragged, waving the knickers under Rod's nose.

"Who the fucks he?" asked Rod.

"Don't know, but apparently, he fucked three of them" I said.

"More like he's been around camp finding lost knickers" said Rod.

"No really, I fucked them", he said.

"Ah! Fuck off to shit house and wank tha sen silly yer lying bastard" said Rod.

"I'm not lying" said the lad.

"Let's have a look at them then" said Rod, grabbing the knickers.

He unfolded them, sniffed at them and inspected the crotch area.

"There clean, there's no fanny juice or owt on them, so fuck off" he said, throwing the knickers back at the lad.

"You're a fuckin animal" I said to Rod.

"Bollocks" he replied.

"You should have come up to the radio room" I said.

"Is that where you went with Jeanie?" he asked.

"Yep and guess what, she's still up there, and that's not all, one of the missing girls is up there as well. I've only come down here to get some food and then I'm going back to them" I explained.

"Randy bastard, you got two up there, I'm coming back up with you." he said.

I explained to him that Lin was not exactly a friend of Jeanie's so I didn't know how she would react to him being there, so for once in his life could he treat a girl with a little respect, he agreed and we made our way up to the radio room.

Back in the radio room I introduced them, they seemed to be getting on alright, he was over the moon when he saw that she was Eurasian and I have never heard him be so nice and polite in all the time I had known him.

Jeanie on the other hand looked at me as if I had walked in with shit on my shoe.

They must really have liked each other because a while later they both disappeared into the backroom and I could hear the springs on the old bed squeaking, they also started seeing each other on a regular basis and he seemed like a changed man.

It must be love.

We did eventually leave camp that evening by taxi, just as it was starting to get dark, we just drove straight past the guardroom and out of the gates without stopping.

"Anyone want to write to my sister back in the UK? She wants a pen pal" announced Rod.

"Not if she's an ugly git like you" said Frank.

No one offered so I said,

"Go on then, give me her address I'll write to her".

"Is she the one that does things to Mars bars" asked Frank.

"Fuck off you" he said, scowling at Frank.

"Sarge is going to write to her".

He passed me a piece of paper with her name and address written on it.

"Angela, nice name" I commented.

"And don't go writing owt mucky to her she's only fifteen" he said.

"Yer, fifteen now, but she'll be sixteen by the time you get back to the UK later this year, Sarge" said Frank.

I wrote to her, and received a reply about a week later, she seemed like a nice girl from what she was saying in her letters, but you can write anything when your thousands of miles away, can't you. We continued to write to each other and I knew just about everything there was to know about her except the colour of her underwear, and I think she would have told me that if I had asked her.

Some of her letters were getting very serious, she even said she was falling in love with me, how can that be, we have never meet.

Red walked into the barrack room, which usually meant that he had a job for someone, some of the lads saw him coming and without warning us, they ran into the toilet block out of the way.

"Sarge, you'll do and you" he said, pointing to Frank.

"Got a little job for you" he continued, "Come with me".

"Ah! For fucks sake" said Frank, under his breath.

"Where we going Sir" I asked.

"To the transport yard, you're going on 'Rebro 88' " he replied.

Now Rebro 88 was short for Rebroadcast Station call sign Eight Eight, which meant we had to sit on top of Victoria Peak in a Land Rover for the next twenty four hours manning two radios, so that the lads from the other companies could talk to control, while they were on patrol on Lantau Island on some kind of good will exercise.

This was one of those jobs we used to hate.

Trying to get out of it I said,

"But what about the radio room in the morning Sir".

"Give your keys to" he looked to see who was left in the room, "To him", pointing at Rod, "He can make the call" he said.

Now this cheered Rod up no end, he had been trying to get his hands on the keys so he could take Lin up there anytime he wanted.

I had, had some copies made of the keys, I took one off the key ring and reluctantly threw it towards him he caught it and rubbed his hands together.

"Bastard" I mumbled.

"Shagging tonight" he said.

"Don't go making a mess up there", I said, following Red out of the door.

At the transport yard I was issued and had to sign for a Land Rover.

"Why do I have to sign for it?" I asked.

"Because you're now a driver radio operator" replied Red.

"Gee, thanks Sir, just what I've always wanted" I said, being sarcastic.

"Good, well you've got it then haven't you" he said, being sarcastic back.

'Great', I thought, 'Just what I needed, something else to clean and look after'.

We then reported to our stores where we fitted two radios into the back and were given our orders for Vicky Peak.

On the way there we stopped off at a phone box and Frank rang the flat to tell Lily and Jeanie why we couldn't go to them, and asked them to come up the peak and join us for the night they agreed to meet us later that afternoon, so it wasn't going to be a bad night after all.

We arrived parked at the far end away from the tourists, erected our two twenty seven foot masts and radio antennas, tuned in the radios, connected them together in rebro and made the first call.

'Hello zero alpha this is eight eight radio check over'
'Zero alpha OK over'
'Eight eight OK out'

Frank made a call on the other radio.

'Hello zero this is eight eight radio check over'
'Zero OK over'

'Eight eight OK out'

Frank switched on the rebro, which effectively took over from us, and I contacted both stations

'Hello all stations this is eight eight'
'You have rebro out'

The two stations could now speak directly to each other and providing nothing went wrong with any of the equipment that was it , bored out of our skulls for the next twenty four hours, well at least until the girls arrived.

It's strange how when your one your own with someone, how one of you starts talking about things that you would not normally say or discuss with anyone, and for some reason Frank was very talkative.

"You know what I'm going to do" he said.

"Go on what?" I asked, sat with my feet up on the dash of the Land Rover, listening to the hum of the radio just behind my head, and not really taking any notice of him.

"Get married" he said calmly.

"Get married, who the fuck to" I asked?" jumping up straight.

"Lily" he replied.

"Lily, are you sure" I asked.

"I asked her and she said yes" he said.

"What about her parents, have you met them?" I asked.

"Yes, they have no objections" he said.

"Well what about the army, they won't let you marry a Chinese girl, will they?" I said.

"I've spoke to the C.O, and the Padre, they have asked me if I'm sure I know what I'm doing, and have given me permission, well actually they can't stop me" he said.

"Do the girls know about this yet?" I asked.

"Not unless Lily as told them" he replied.

Are you sure that Lily is not just using you to get a passport to the UK?" I asked.

"No she already has a UK passport and anyway she wants to stay here in Hong Kong, so I'm thinking about buying myself out of the army and staying here with her" he said.

"What will you do for a living?" I asked.

"Probably join the Hong Kong Police Force" he said.

"So what's the problem, are you having second thoughts about marrying her?" I asked.

"No, I love her and I want to marry her, but she comes from a poor family and I don't have a great deal of savings, well not enough to pay for a wedding and buy myself out of the army and find somewhere for us to live" he explained.

"You love the girl and she loves you, right?" I asked.

"Right" he replied.

"You both want to get married, right?" I asked.

"Right" he replied again.

"So problem solved" I said, waiting for his reaction.

"How is it solved?" he asked.

"I will pay for the wedding and give you the money to buy you out, and then you can use your money to find somewhere to live, call it a wedding present" I said.

"Don't talk so fuckin daft, and where are you getting the money from?" he asked.

"Don't worry about it, do you want it or not?" I asked.

"Explain to me first how you can afford it?" he asked

I explained my circumstances to him and after he got over the shock he reluctantly agreed, provided that I agreed to be his best man.

"OK, then sorted, you get on with all the arrangements" I said pulling my cheque book out of my pocket and writing a cheque out.

"Will five thousand pound cover it, if not let me know and you can have some more", I said, handing the cheque to him.

"Thanks Sarge, if you were a girl, I'd kiss you" he said.

"If I were a girl and you kissed me and Lily found out you wouldn't be getting married" I said.

"Hey! There are two girls walking this way shall we chat them up" said Frank, looking out of the side window of the Land Rover.

"You leave them alone, you're nearly a married man" I said, leaning forward to look past him at the girls.

"You can have the one on the right, I'll have the other" he said.

"Jeanie's on the left, you're not having her, Lily will kill you" I said, laughing.

"Get your tits out for the lads" Frank shouted at them.

"OK" said Jeanie, unbuttoning her top.

"Behave you" I said.

I jumped into the back of the Land Rover with Jeanie and Lily got in the front with Frank.

"I hear congratulations are in order" I said to Lily.

"Frank told you?" she asked.

"Yes" I replied "But what do you want to marry this ugly bugger for, when you could have a handsome devil like me" I joked.

"Because I love him" she said.

"Did you know?" I asked Jeanie.

"We only found out today" she replied.

Frank at this point told Lily that I was paying for the wedding, and showed her the cheque.

Lily couldn't believe what Frank was saying, the look on her face was amazing and Jeanie was even more astonished.

I then got the How's, Where's, and Why's from both girls, so I explained my circumstances to them, that was it my secret was out of the bag, but would it make any difference to Jeanie, only time will tell.

"Hey Sarge, you want to marry me?" asked Jeanie.

"Is that a proposal?" I asked her.

"Yes" she replied.

"No" I said.

"Good, I don't want to marry you either" she said, touching the dials on front of one of the radios.

Leave my knob alone, you'll break it" I said.

"What are you two on about?" asked Frank.

"She's playing with my knob" I replied, knocking her hand away from the radio.

"Tell her to leave it alone or it will drop off" laughed Frank.

"I will play with your nob" she said, grabbing me between the legs.

"Ouch, that hurt" I shouted, shoving my hand up her skirt between her legs, to get my own back.

"Wooooo! I like that" she said, trapping my hand with her thighs and pushing her hips forwards.

"You always do" I said.

"That's why you like me" she said, holding my arm with both her hands so I couldn't pull my hand back out from under her skirt.

"Frank listen to the radio, I'm going for a walk with Jeanie" I said.

"OK! Have fun" he replied.

That summer Frank and Lily were married in the little church on the camp, the service was conducted by the army Padre and everything went very smoothly considering that most of us were suffering with hangovers from Frank's stag do the night before.

He eventually bought himself out of the army and joined the Hong Kong Police; they found a nice little flat, just around the corner from Island Pol Mil the main police and military headquarters in Victoria.

After the wedding, Justin wanted to talk to me, he seemed very anxious, as if he had some kind of problem, so I took him to the Hilton where I knew we wouldn't be disturbed, and we had a meal in the restaurant.

"You know how we are going back to the UK in a few months" he said.

"Yer! That's good isn't it" I said.

"No, not really I don't want to go" he said.

"I don't think I do, but there's nothing we can do about it, unless we do what Frank's just done, and there's no way I'm marrying Jeanie and you certainly can't marry Tammy" I said.

"There is one thing that we have been considering" he said.

"Go on" I said.

"We were considering that I should buy myself out of the army and buy a bar in Wan Chai, but we can't do it on our own, we need someone else to invest money in it with us" he said.

"And that's where I come in?" I asked.

"Yes" he replied.

I asked him lots of other questions about cost, profit, turnover, and how much money he was talking about but he didn't have the answers.

"Look" I said, "Find out the information you need and I will consider it".

We sat eating our meal when Red and Mercedes walked in.

I didn't know she was back in Hong Kong, 'must be on holiday again' I thought

"Oh! Christ, look who's just walked in" I said.

"Come on let's get out of here quick" said Justin.

"Too late they've seen us" I said.

"Hello John" said Mercedes, walking passed me.

"Hello, are you on holiday again?" I asked.

"Yes" she replied and sat down with Red at a table across the room from us.

"What's with the hello again do you know her?" asked Justin.

I explained who she was and about what had happened that night in the radio room.

"And you didn't fuck her" whispered Justin.

"No, and now Red thinks I'm the perfect gentleman and the sun shines out of my arse" I said.

"Platoon Commanders proper little blue eyed boy, aren't we" said Justin, taking the piss.

"Yer! But she's a year older now, so the first chance I get I'm going to shag the arse off her" I said, looking across the room at Mercedes, who saw me and smiled back.

"Yep! You're in there my son, look at her she's practically asking for it" he said.

When we had finish our meal, I paid the bill and sent a bottle of Champagne over to Red's table with my compliments, I had to get in there somehow if I were going to get another chance with Mercedes.

We were getting up to leave when the waiter came back with the message, would I like to go over and join them.

"See I told you, you were in there, I'll see you later" said Justin, and he left.

I went over and sat next to Mercedes at their table, not really knowing what to say.

"I've still got your shoes", I blurted out like an idiot.

"Have you, I was wondering where they were", she said, looking at me as if I were the village idiot, we both burst out laughing.

"What were you two chaps doing here?" asked Red, butting in.

"Just enjoying a meal, Sir" I replied.

"Please drop the 'Sir' and call me Roger" he said.

'Well slap me legs and call me Roger' I thought.

"Quite expensive, but very nice" he continued.

"Yes, Sir, sorry, Sir, Roger Sir, force of habit Sir, I'm not used to calling officers by their Christian name" I stuttered.

"Oh! Uncle he's so funny", said Mercedes, laughing out loud, has she put her hand on my leg under the table.

"Don't worry about it Sarge, it would probably be better if you stuck to sir, we don't want you calling me Roger on camp, do we" he said.

We sat and talked for a while and I got the distinct impression that he was playing matchmaker.

The bill arrived and I picked it up.

"I'll get this, Sir" I said.

"No don't be silly" he said, but he was too late, I already had it in my hand.

"No sir, I insist" I said, putting the money on the tray.

"Alright if you insist, I will get it next time" he said.

'Next time, is he planning a next time' I thought.

"Come on Mercedes, your aunt will be waiting for us" he said.

Oh! Uncle can't I stay with John, he will look after me, won't you?" she asked, looking at me and squeezing my leg.

Red studied awhile and said.

"OK, I'll leave you two kids together, I am sure you can find something to amuse yourself with" he said.

'Yer, too right we can' I thought.

"Right what would you like to do first?" I asked her.

"Go to bed with you, go and book a room" she said.

'Well there's nothing like getting straight to the point' I thought.

"I already have a suite here" I said.

"Well what are we waiting for, you want to go to bed with me don't you?" she said.

"Oh! Yes" I replied, grabbing her hand and heading for the lift.

On the way up to the suite in the lift, she was all over me, kissing and rubbing herself up against me.

"Come on lift, you slow thing" she said, stamping her foot on the floor like a spoilt child.

"Calm down, take your time" I said.

"No, I want you now, I've waited a year for this" she demand.

We entered the suite and made straight for the bedroom, she was stripping off her clothes as she went, and was completely naked by the time we got to the bed, she pulled me down on top of her, while tearing at my clothes to get them off.

"Wait, we need a condom" I said.

"Forget the condom" she said.

"Why are you on the pill?" I asked.

"No, just fuck me will you" she said, getting annoyed.

"No way, no condom no sex" I said, the last thing I wanted to do was make her pregnant.

"In my bag and hurry" she said.

I retrieved her bag from the floor where she had dropped it, there were enough condoms in her bag to keep the whole regiment happy.

"What flavour would you like?" I asked, joking,

I turned to go back to the bed and could see she was now rubbing herself between the legs.

"Any flavour you like, just get one on and get back over here before it's too late", she said.

I moved her hand out of the way and pulled her to the edge of the bed, and entered her, while I was still stood on the floor next to the bed, she hooked her legs around my back and I pushed into her, within seconds we reached an orgasm together. We stayed like that for a few minutes then I felt her orgasm again, she arched her back and pushed herself upwards onto me, afterwards we lay on the bed together with our arms around each other.

"What flavour was it anyway?" she asked.

"Does it matter, blackcurrant ribbed, I think" I said.

"I know it was ribbed, I could feel it" she said.

We settled down to a few hours of love making, she couldn't stay all night otherwise Red would be looking for her, and I did see her a few more times before the end of her holiday and she returned to England.

Justin got back to me with the details about the bar investment, this time he knew what he was talking about, and had arranged for me to go with him to view a bar.

The bar, which name I won't reveal, was a grubby run down place on Wan Chai's main street, but then again they all were, I spent every night for the next week or so just sitting in the place, I suppose you could call it a reconnaissance exercise.

Jeanie wasn't pleased because I was in a bar all night with the bar girls around me, but once she found out what I was doing she relented and stopped nagging me about it.

Justin had arranged for us to see a solicitor who drew up a contract, making me part owner, I didn't have anything to do with the running of the business, I left that to Justin and Tammy.

Anyway everything got signed, I handed over my part of the money, Justin bought himself out of the army and opened the bar.

It stayed a prosperous investment, and I collected profits from it every year until it was sold in 1997, when Hong Kong was given back to China.

As far as I know Justin and Tammy, moved on and bought another business, they still live in Hong Kong, but I haven't had anything to do with then since the bar closed.

In September 1970 with only a few more months before the regiment came back to England, I was summoned one evening to attend the officers mess, I had to report to Red,

I didn't know what for, had he found out that I'd been having sex with Mercedes.

I reported to the Corporal at the desk inside the entrance and was directed to a small office at the side where Red was waiting for me.

"Sit down Sarge" he said, as I entered the office.

I did as I was told and sat down still wondering what the hell he wanted me for.

"I'm sorry son, but I am the bearer of bad news" he continued.

'What the hell's going on, first he calls me Sarge, but he always did, and now he's calling me son' I thought.

"We have just received a message from England that your mother is very seriously ill and is not expected to live through the night" he said.

I felt like someone had just hit me with a ton of bricks, I didn't know she was ill, let alone dying, I knew I hadn't had any letters from her for awhile, but I thought nothing about it, and none of my family had wrote to me to let me know, my head was in turmoil, too many questions, why?, what?, when?, I just didn't know what to say to him.

"She can't be dying, she's only fifty" I blurted out.

Red passed the paper with the message on over to me, I read it and somehow it became more real.

"You are flying back to the UK in four hours, I will pick you up in two hours outside your barrack block and take you to the airport, you will collect your ticket from the check in, and you cannot leave your kit behind, so go and pack it now, because you're not coming back to Hong Kong, you can change any currency you have at the airport and don't forget your passport.

I hadn't really heard a word he had just said to me.

'Airport, passport, money, pack, mother, what to do next? Jeanie, Hilton, two hours, and too many things' my head was spinning, and at this point I was close to tears.

"Sir if I leave you a blank cheque made out to the Hilton will you check me out and pay them for me, I don't have time" I said.

"You have a room at the Hilton?" he asked.

"Yes, Sir, please will you do it for me?" I asked.

"Yes, I will" he replied.

"Thank you, sir, that's one less thing to worry about" I said, filling the cheque out and passing it to him.

"Just fill in the amount that I owe them" I said.

"Right, you go and get your kit packed, I will see you at eight, you fly at ten" he said, looking at his watch.

Back in the barrack room I packed my kit, the lads wanted to know what I was doing, so I past them the message that Red had given me and let them read it for themselves.

"Oh! For fucksake" said Rod.

"Come on, let's help you pack", said Billy, who actually knew my mother, I could see tears in his eyes and I tried not to look directly at him, knowing I would break down if I did.

My kit was packed, the lads said they would hand in any other stuff I had back at the stores for me, so that saved me another job. I sat and wrote a letter to Jeanie explaining what had happened and asked her to write to me.

"Will you tell Justin and Frank what's happened and give this letter to Jeanie for me" I said to Billy.

"No problem mate, consider it done" he said.

"I've just got to go and get something I have forgotten" I said, remembering Mercedes shoes in the radio room.

When I arrived back I packed them in my case.

"Here Rod" I said, throwing him all the keys to the radio room.

"Don't forget to ask Red if you can keep them" I added.

At 8pm Red picked me up outside the block in the C.O's staff car, I threw my case and kit bag in the boot, turned and waved at Rod and Billy who were on the balcony looking down at me, then I got into the car.

"Let me know how she is" shouted Billy.

"See you at Catterick" shouted Rod.

Catterick Garrison was where the Dukes were to be stationed on their arrival back in England.

I checked in at the airport, I had the best part of two hours to wait before my flight, Red asked if I wanted him to stay with me until then, I told him no I would be alright on my own. Thinking about my mother, I hadn't seen her since I was last in England the best part of two and a half years ago, then it dawned on me, Hong Kong is eight hours in front of the UK, I looked at my watch, it's 9pm here now, so it's 1pm in the UK on the 19th September, I took the message out of my pocket and read the date, it was dated in London on the 18th September. 'Yesterday', I'm going to be too late by the time I get home, I have to fly to England then catch a train up to Yorkshire' I thought.

"Sarge" someone shouted.

I looked up and running towards me was Jeanie.

'Oh! No, I can't handle this' I thought.

"Sarge" she shouted again, flinging her arms around my neck and kissing me.

"Billy just told me, I'm so sorry", she said with tears streaming down her cheeks.

That was it, I just couldn't take anymore, my mother was dying, I didn't know if I would make it home in time to see her again, I had to leave my girl behind, I cracked up in front of everyone there.

We found a quiet corner and stood with our arms around each other kissing until my flight was called.

"Did Billy give you my letter?" I asked her.

"Yes" she replied, sobbing.

"My address is on it, write to me" I said.

"I will" she said.

The tannoy announced it was time to board my flight.

I lifted her head and kissed her on the lips.

"I love you" I said.

"I know and I love you too, don't forget me, will you" she replied.

"No, I'll never forget you" I replied.

She walked with me, holding my hand towards the departure gate, then she let go, turned and walked away.

"Bye" she said.

"Bye" I said, watching her go.

"I'll come back for you, I promise" I shouted after her, but she didn't look back.

She knew we would never meet again, and somehow, somewhere deep in my heart, I knew I wouldn't keep my promise to come back for her.

Looking back through the plane window as it took off.

'Bye Jeanie, I love you, Bye'.

I arrived home in the early hours of the next morning and as I had predicted I was too late my mother had passed away on the 18th, before I even knew about it.

I didn't stay at home, though my father and other members of my family wanted me to, now my mother had gone, there just didn't seem to be a reason for me to be there anymore, so I booked into a local hotel, and laid awake on the bed, I just couldn't get Jeanie out of my head.

After the funeral I was really at a loose end, I had been given compassionate leave and my normal leave which were running back to back; I didn't have to report to Catterick until January.

I called my old mate Willie Wanker, but he was now married and his wife didn't like the idea of me taking him to the pub and Tosser was now in the RAF.

Then I remembered Angela, Rod's sister, I had been writing to her for the best part of a year, and she didn't know yet that I was now back in the country. I went back home and took my car back from my sister who had been running it for me while I was away, she wasn't best pleased when I told her I wanted my it back and reluctantly handed over the keys, when my father promised to buy her one.

I drove to Rod's home town and found the estate a dreary looking place of five high rise blocks of flats with rubbish strewn in the streets, I was wondering if it was safe to leave my car and would it have any wheels left on it when I returned.

I found the block I was searching for and entered the building, pushed the button on the lift to go up to the tenth floor, nothing happened.

"That don't work mate" said a young lad of about thirteen with his arms around a girl who looked even younger, in the corner of the stairwell.

"Cheers" I said and proceeded to climb the stairs.

"Who tha looking for anyrooded?" he asked.

"Number twenty" I said.

"Hey, that's your house" said the girl to the boy.

"Aye it is, if tha'ra bailiff, my mam in't in" he said.

"I'm not a bailiff, I'm looking for Angela" I said.

"Hey! It's him, that new posh bloke your Angie's been writing to" said the girl.

"Ha tha?" asked the lad.

"Am I what?" I asked.

"That posh git ar Angie's been writing to" he said.

"Aye a, am" I said, in my best Yorkshire accent, and with that he ran upstairs with the girl, I assume to give Angela warning that I was on my way.

After climbing, what seemed an endless mountain of stairs?

I finally arrived at the tenth floor, to be greeted by a hoard of people. 'This lot can't all be Rod's family' I thought, apparently the lad had been and told all the neighbours that I was here and they had also come out to see me.

"Come in lad, mek tha sen at home" said a large round lady, who I imagine was Rod's mother.

I entered the flat it was like a dump it site, the sort of place where you had to wipe your feet before you left.

No, I'm being unfair; the place wasn't dirty, it just that everything look old worn out and thread bare.

"Sit darn a'll mek us a cuppa tea" said the woman.

"Don't bother thanks, I don't drink tea" I said.

"Here tha'ar then, get this darn tha" said a middle aged guy, who I assumed was Rod's father, sat in a beat up old armchair, holding his hand out with a can of beer in it.

"No thanks, I'm driving", I said, wondering where on earth Angela was.

"Whe're tha motor?" asked the lad looking over the balcony.

"Is tha it, that red Poorsher", it'll get nick round here" he said, then everyone went to look down at the car.

"Get tha sen away from that motor", he shouted to some kids who were playing nearby.

"Here, give us a quid, and I'll look after it for tha" he said.

Thinking this may be the lesser of two evils, one I get rid of him and two I get the car looked after, so I gave him a pound and he left.

The next time I looked over at the car, he was sat on the bonnet. 'That'll do the paint work a lot of good', I thought.

I was getting sick of waiting, and was in two minds if I should leave or not.

"Where's Angela?" I asked.

"She's at work lad she'll be home soon" said Rod's father.

"What time?" I asked.

"In abart half an hour, does she know tha were coming, cos she didn't say owt to us" said Rod's mother.

"That's the problem she doesn't even know I am back from Hong Kong yet, I was sent home early because my mother had died" I explained.

"Did tha hear that Dorothy, his Mams died so t' army sent him home" said Rod's father.

"Aye, Fred I heard him, poor lad" said Dorothy.

"So tha's come to see ar Angie as tha, well she'll look after tha, when she gets home, she's a good lass" said Fred.

"Here Sally, go and look for Angie, tell her to hurry cos someone's waiting to see her" said Dorothy, looking at a young girl aged about twelve, who was sat next to me on the sofa, when she got older, the poor girl was nicknamed 'Mustang' by the local lads, because they said it was like riding a bucking bronco.

"Who shall a tell her it is, Mam?" asked Sally.

"Tell her it's Sarge" I said.

"Sarge is that tha real name or tha rank in't t'army?" asked Fred

"It's my nickname, my surname is Sargeant so everyone calls me Sarge, my first name is John" I replied.

The door opened and in ran Sally.

"She's coming nar Mam" she said.

A few moments later Angela walked in.

"Hi Mam" she said, kissing her mother on the cheek.

"Had a good day love?" asked her mother.

"Aye" she replied.

"Say hello to Sarge then, he's come all t'way from Hong Kong to see tha" said, Fred.

"Shuuurup dad, don't be so daft, he's not come all the way from Hong Kong, just to see me" she said.

"No lass, his Mams died" said Dorothy.

Angela looked a great girl, long blond hair, green eyes and a nice little figure she was wearing a T shirt and a very short mini skirt with legs all the way up to her armpits, if you know what I mean, it was a pity really, because from her background, she was probably destined to have six kids and a council house.

"Hi" she said, blushing slightly.

"Hi" I replied.

We sat and talked for awhile getting to know each other and I explained why I had suddenly turned up out of the blue, without any warning.

"Come on, let's go out" she said, putting her coat on.

I just followed her out through the door, down the stairs and out into the car park., where her brother was still sitting on my car.

"Get off that car, before someone see's you" said Angela,

"It's his, am looking after it for him" he said, pointing at me.

"What, this is yours?" she asked, looking at the car.

"I'm afraid so" I replied, opening the car door for her.

"Get in" I said.

It was plain to see that she hadn't got a clue how a girl wearing a mini skirt should enter a sports car without losing her dignity.

'Nice, black, very sexy' I thought, enjoying the scenery, until she looked up and noticed I was looking directly up her skirt, not very gentlemanly, I know, well I am only human, she quickly tried to cover herself by pulling her skirt down, but there wasn't much skirt to pull down, even sat straight in the seat she was still showing her knickers, realising she was fighting a losing battle with the skirt she finally gave up and accepted it.

"I don't know the area, so where do you want to go?" I asked, getting into the driver's seat.

"Just drive around for now" she replied.

We must have driven around for a couple of hours, just talking and getting to know each other, I don't know what she thought about me, but I was relaxed and enjoying her company, she told me she was sixteen and worked part time as a shop assistant in the local store near where she lived.

She asked me where I was from and about my life in the army some of her questions were a little difficult to answer. 'Like how come I had a flash motor, how come I was wearing a suit, and I come I spoke with a posh accent', well posh compared to hers, she explained.

It was clear that she didn't know my circumstances, Rod couldn't tell her because as far as I knew, he didn't know, so I didn't tell her, so as far as she was concerned I was just a mate of her brothers who was in the army.

"Shall we stop and get something to eat?" I asked.

"If you like, where we going, for a burger?" she asked.

"If that's what you want" I replied.

She must have been thinking, I was taking her to the local burger bar, because she started giving me directions.

I pulled into a large restaurant car park on the main road just outside town.

"This will do" I said.

"I can't go in there" she complained.

"Of course you can, come on" I said, I got out of the car went around to the passenger side and opened the door for her.

"Don't look up my skirt this time" she said, blushing.

"I'm sorry, but you can't blame me, can you" I said.

"No, you can't help it, can you, you're a bloke" she said.

"Look do it this way, keep your legs together, now swing your body around and swing both your legs out of the car at the same time then stand up, and when you get back in the car, do the same thing in reverse" I explained.

I never thought I would hear myself telling a girl to keep her legs together, but I suppose there is a first time for everything.

She did as I had instructed and retained her dignity, although I liked the other method she had for getting in and out of a car, but then I would, wouldn't I.

Inside the restaurant I ordered the meal and a bottle of house wine, which she seemed to really enjoy.

"Enjoying it?" I asked.

"I would have settled for a burger and a can of pop" she said, blushing again.

"You've got one" I said, pointing to the burger on her plate.

"I feel out of place in here, look at everyone their all dressed up" she said.

"Look, don't worry you have as much right to be in here as any of these people" I said, nodding my head towards the others who were dining.

"That guy over there is even picking his nose" I whispered

"Shuuurup, yer daft devil" she laughed.

"You look fine, I could take you anywhere twice" I said.

"Yer, the second time to apologise" she said.

"Stop worrying" I said.

"Yer! But, look, their all dressed up and look at the state of me, even you have a suit on" she said, tugging at her top.

"You look great to me" I said, putting my hand on hers across the table.

"Next time you bring me somewhere like this, let me know first so I can get dolled up a bit" she said.

"So there's going to be a next time then?" I asked.

"Oh, certainly, you're a swathe, sophisticated young gentleman in a suit with a flash motor, how can I refuse" she said in a posh voice, laughing and taking the piss.

We finished our meal and went back out to the car, I opened the door for her and she remembered what I had said about her legs.

Oh, why did I have to open my big mouth?

"Where would you like to go now?" I asked.

"Anywhere" she replied.

I sat looking across at her, now she had really relaxed, she looked stunning, the little dimples in her cheeks when she smiled, and those amazing green eyes, she was beautiful.

"Can I kiss you?" I asked.

"Most lads don't ask" she said turning towards me, I leaned over and kissed her softly on the lips, she put her arms around my neck, looked into my eyes and we kissed again, I let my hand drop onto her leg and rubbed her thigh very lightly.

' Tights' I thought, how strange it felt, I hadn't touched the smooth silky legs of a girl wearing tights for a long time, in Hong Kong the girls didn't wear them.

Still kissing, I moved my hand up her legs.

"No", she said, grabbing my hand, which I removed straight away.

"Don't do that" she said.

"I'm sorry" I said, what was I doing, usually if I got that far with a girl it was too late to stop me.

"I don't want to do that yet" she said.

"It's alright; I'm not going to force you into doing anything you don't want to do" I replied kissing her again.

"I'm sorry" she said.

"Sorry what for?" I asked.

"For not doing it with you, you've been so nice to me and I want to give you something in return" she said.

"Maybe, but you don't have to give me your body" I said.

"No, I want to, but I'm scared" she said.

"Scared of what?" I asked, without thinking.

"Just scared" she replied.

"Scared of getting pregnant, don't worry about that I've got some condoms" I said, I still hadn't realised what she was trying to tell me.

"No, scared of doing it, you know, it" she said again.

Then like a bolt out of the blue, I realised.

"You're still a virgin, aren't you?" I asked.

"Yes" she sobbed, with tears filling her eyes.

'How she had managed to get to sixteen and remain a virgin in the area she lived in is a mystery, there seemed to be young couples in every stairwell going at it for all they were worth.

"Don't Cry, you silly girl" I said, trying to comfort her.

"I'm sorry" she said.

"Listen, if you really want to have sex for the first time and you want me to be the one, then let me sort somewhere nice for us to go, you're not losing your virginity in a car, I want it to be special for you" I said.

I think I'm falling in love with you" she said.

"I know, you said so in your letters" I replied, kissing her.

We sat kissing and cuddling in the car for the rest of the evening.

Later I drove her home, she asked me in but I declined the thought of spending more time with her family just didn't appeal to me. I booked into a local hotel so I could be near her, and arranged to see her again the next day, and the next day, and the next day after that.

She wasn't working at the weekend so I booked a long weekend stay at a large hotel in York, miles away from her home town, and so they didn't suspect anything I asked her parents if it was alright for her to come with me to visit my family and stay for the weekend.

All her father said was "I don't know why tha asking lad, she can go where she wants, she's sixteen".

They didn't seem to care what I did or where I took their daughter, so after that I took him at his word and she was very rarely at home.

On the Friday evening we drove to York most of the way there I drove with one hand, my other hand was on her leg.

"Look in glove box" I said to her.

"What am I looking for?" she asked.

"A ring box put the ring on your third finger" I said.

It was the ring I once bought Jeanie that she refused to accept from me.

"No way, we're not married, it's bad luck" she said.

"Put it on, I've booked us into the hotel as Mr and Mrs Sargeant, and we have to look like newlyweds or they won't let us stay there" I explained.

"You get away with murder, you do" she said, slipping the ring on her finger.

Look it doesn't matter who you are or what you do if you're bold enough to act and look the part you can get away with anything, anywhere", I said, hoping to get her off the subject before she started asking how I could afford it.

"And you certainly look the part" she said.

"Yer, don't look too bad yourself" I said.

We arrived at the hotel and parked in their private car park, I opened the door for her and she got out of the car the old way showing her panties.

"I thought that would make you smile" she said, laughing.

"Black again I see, you only got one pair?" I asked

"Cheeky bugger" she said, giving me a playful slap.

"Come on Mrs Sargeant, let's get you seen to" I said.

"Oh! I'm going to get seen to, am I" she said.

"You certainly are madam" I said, grabbing our overnight bags and hitting her on the bum with one.

We were supposed to be newlyweds and we were definitely acting the part.

We checked in at the desk, she was linking my arm with her head leaning on my shoulder while I signed the register.

"Thank you Sir, there are your keys, the bridal suite is on the top floor, have a nice stay" said the desk clerk.

There was a bottle of champagne and some chocolates, compliments of the management to the newlyweds on the table by the side of the bed. I looked at them thinking, 'Thank god it's not a Mars Bar'.

I took Angela in my arms, we kissed and I slowly undressed her, stood in her bra and panties she was shaking like a leaf.

"Calm down, I'm not going to do anything to you that you don't want me to" I said, holding her close to me.

"I can't help it no other lad has seen me naked before" she replied.

"Your beautiful" I said, unhooking her bra and letting it fall away from her breasts.

"Let's get in bed" I said.

She removed her panties and got into bed, covering herself with the sheet she watched me has I got undressed.

"You are the first lad I've ever seen naked" she said.

"And do you like what you've seen so far?" I asked, getting into bed beside her.

"Not sure, are all lads that big" she asked.

"Yes, I suppose so" I replied.

"It's too big, I'll never take all that?" she said.

"Don't worry, you will" I replied.

We kissed and I ran my hands up and down her body, cupping her breast, squeezing her nipples, and rubbing her, I positioned myself ready to take her.

"Wait" she said.

I stopped, and lay perfectly still on her.

"Will it hurt?" she asked.

"If you don't want to do it, you don't have to" I replied.

"But will it hurt?" she asked again.

"Yes at first, then it will probably feel uncomfortable for a while, then when you get used to it you will like it, I promise" I replied, kissing her again I started to move on top of her as if we were already having sex.

"Is that it" she asked,

"No, but this is" I said, pushing into her.

"Oh! My god no, it hurts, take it out, stop, no don't stop, leave it in", she screamed, the tears wielding up in her eyes.

"Sorry, I warned you it may hurt, but make your mind up, do you want it in or out, or in or out, or in or out", I said, moving inside her to the rhythm of my voice.

"Oh! My god, that was painful, what have you done to me?" she asked.

"You, my girl, are no longer a virgin" I said.

"Mmmmm! I like this", she said, as I continued to move inside her, she started to relax.

"I love you, I'm glad I lost my virginity to you" she said.

I moved faster and felt myself wanting to cum, she tensed up and we both reached orgasm together.

"Oh, I like that, it's warm, what have you done?" she asked.

"I've just cum inside you" I said.

"Wow! It's lovely, so is that what it feels like every time someone cum's inside you?" she asked.

"I can't answer that, I'm a bloke" I replied.

"Oh, yer, you wouldn't know, would you, I'm daft aren't I?" she said, laughing.

"Yer, but your funny and you make me laugh" I replied.

"Oh, god, I won't get pregnant, will I?" she asked, with a look of panic on her face.

"No you won't, I'm using a condom", I replied. We stayed in bed for most of the weekend all our meals were brought up to us by room service. If the hotel management weren't convinced we were newlyweds by now then I didn't know what proof they needed, only a newly married couple would stay in bed this long.

A few weeks later, I was sat in Angela's parent's flat waiting for her to come home from work, when Sally came running in through the door.

"Our Andy's here Mam" she shouted.

"Where?" asked her mother.

"Coming up the stairs" replied Sally.

At that moment Rod walked in through the door, carrying his suitcase, he had just arrived back from Hong Kong.

Andy, Andrew, so that's his real name, 'Why did we call him Rod', I wondered. I had lived with him for the best part of two and half years and I never knew his Christian name.

"Eeee lad, it's good to have yer home again" said his mother, throwing her arms around him and kissing him on the cheek.

"Give up Mam" he said, when he saw me on the sofa.

"Hey up! Sarge, what tha doing here?" he asked.

"He's our Angie's fella" Sally blurted out, before I had a chance to answer.

"What? Tha knocking our Angie off" he said.

"I'm afraid so" I replied.

"Well fuck me, the jammy little buggers really dropped on her feet this time" he said.

"Stop swearing Andrew" said his mother.

"Why what's up?" I asked, hoping that he hadn't found out about me and was about to spill the beans.

"She's only gone and gorra sen a fuckin millionaire" he said.

"Rod no, I was going to tell them in my own time, how did you find out?" I asked, looking around at his mother and Sally who were stood with their mouths open in total disbelief.

Tammy and Justin, they told me about the bar and that you paid for Franks wedding and stuff, then Billy said he thought you were or if you weren't you weren't far off being one, but I didn't believe them, so is it's true then or what?" he asked.

"It's true" I replied, there didn't seem to be any point in denying it any longer.

"How are Monica and Jeanie?" I asked, trying to get him off the subject.

"I'll tell you about it later" he replied, winking at me while trying not to let the others see him.

"Does our Angie know?" asked her mother.

"No, I haven't told her" I said.

"Get lost, yer liar, he's not a millionaire, he'd not be with our Angie if he were", said Sally.

"What tha doing in t'army if tha a millionaire?" asked his mother.

"That's what I wanna know?" asked Rod.

"Look wait until Angela gets home and I will explain everything to you" I said.

Just then door opened and she walked in with her dad.

After they had greeted Rod and welcomed him back to the family he said,
"Sit down Sarge's got something to say".

"What's tha want lad, to marry our Angie? No problem tha can have her" said his dad.

"Dad be quiet, and listen" said Angela.

"I've been keeping a secret from everyone" I said.

"You're not married are you?" asked Angela, looking as if she was about to burst into tears.

"No he's not married, now listen its important" said Rod.

"I've got a secret" I said again.

"He's a millionaire" Sally blurted out.

"Get lost" said Angela.

"It's true" I said looking at her. "I'm sorry I should have at least told you".

"I don't believe you" she said.

"Look I'll start from the beginning, my name is John Thomas Sargeant I was born in ....

Now I'm here and you know the rest, so please don't ask any more questions" I said, feeling like my world was about to end, I knew Angela would probably dump me regardless of who I was, I knew she would be thinking that people would think she was only going with me for my money, and this was one reason why I didn't want them to know, at that moment in time I hated being a millionaire.

"Now we know why he's got a flash motor" said Sally.

Angela didn't say a word she looked at me as if I had just admitted to a murder or was a rapist, and then went to her room.

"What's up with her? I wish my boyfriend were a millionaire" said Sally.

"Tha shouldn't have a boyfriend thy age" said her dad.

"I think I'd better go" I said.

"No lad, she'll, be back in a bit when she gets over the shock" said her mother.

"Come on mate, let's go down to the pub, tell her where we are Mam and that she's got to come down to us" said Rod.

In the pub the conversation got around to our time in Hong Kong and the girls.

"So how are Jeanie and the girls?" I asked.

"Well! You're a superstar now" he replied.

"What are you on about?" I asked.

"Me, you and Billy, are porn stars now, the girls had cameras hidden in their rooms and the bathroom, they were making blue movies, then selling them to the brothels and those little back street cinemas" he replied.

"Don't be so daft" I said.

"It's true, Justin told me. Jeanie and Monica were using us to make porno, that's how they earned a living" he laughed.

"For Christ sake, don't tell you're Angela, will you?" I said looking at my watch and wondering why she hadn't joined us.

"Don't worry mate I won't say anything and stop looking at your watch Angie will be here soon" he said.

"I hope so" I replied.

"You really do like our Angie, don't you?"

"Is it that obvious" I replied.

"Well there's no accounting for taste" he laughed.

"Ha, ha, very funny" I replied.

We had a few more drinks and talked about the girls in Hong Kong. Angela didn't turn up so I assumed that it was over between us. Rod went home, he offered me the sofa for the night but I couldn't stay there with Angela in the next room. I went back to my hotel.

I drove into our barracks at Catterick and was directed to my barrack block and parked just behind it, found myself a bed in the corner as always, and drew some bedding from the stores, I was the only one in that room at the moment, but knew later that some more of the lads would be returning from leave.

I heard footsteps coming down the corridor and stuck my head around the door to see who it was.

"Hello Sarge, your back nice and early" said Red.

"Yes, sir" I replied.

"How's your mother, is she better now?" he asked.

"No sir she passed away, I didn't get home in time to see her" I said.

"Oh! I am sorry to hear that" he replied.

"Thank you for getting me home anyway, Sir" I said.

"Was that your Porsche I saw come in awhile ago?" he asked.

"Yes sir" I said.

"So is it true what I have heard about you?" he asked.

"Depends what you've heard Sir" I said.

"That you're a very rich young man" he said.

"Yes Sir it's true" I said, thinking 'Oh! To hell with it, let's tell everyone, he didn't say who had told him, he didn't need to I could guess'.

"The C.O may want to see you about it" he said.

"Oh! And before I go here's your receipt from the Hong Kong Hilton and this is for you" he said, handing me the receipt and an envelope, then he left.

I opened the envelope it was a letter from Mercedes, it seems she also knew about me, because her uncle Red had told her, the letter included her phone number and an address and would I like to go and visit her or phone her.

'Yer! Right, I bet she would like to marry a millionaire' I thought.

I did write to her that night explaining that it was only a rumour and that I wasn't a millionaire, I also returned her shoes.

Strange, I never heard from her again, I wonder why.

By now some of the other lads had returned from leave and found themselves a bed, but as yet no one had joined me in this room, so I went to talk to them, and yes you've guess it, they knew about me as well, it now seemed like I was being alienated by them, and looking increasingly like I wasn't one of them anymore, so I went back to my room and laid on my bed, it was at that moment that I decided to buy myself out of the army.

I must have dropped off to sleep, because the next thing I knew was when Rod was shaking me.

"You, you bastard, is there anyone you haven't told about me" I said.

"What do you mean?" he asked.

"Red knows, the C.O knows, the lads know, every fucker and his mother knows, thanks to you" I replied.

"Well you couldn't keep it quiet forever" he said.

"I managed to keep it quiet for nearly six years and now you've fucked it up, I've got to see the C.O tomorrow" I shouted at him.

"He'll probably kick you out" he said.

"Well he's no need to bother I'm going to buy myself out anyway" I said.

"You never did give a proper answer to this question.

"So, what's a bloke like you, with all that money doing in the army?" he asked.

"What's has me being a millionaire got to do with it, it shouldn't matter how much money I have or how much money you have, it's a job, just like any other job, it's a job I like doing, I feel at home in the army, I like being here, it's my family, but now it seems that this family is turning its back on me as well, just like your Angela and everyone else does, when they find out, so fuck the lot of you" I shouted.

"OK, calm down, I understand and our Angela hasn't turned her back on you, she wants you to go and see her" he said.

"Oh she does, does she, well it's taken her long enough to decide" I replied. Rod could see I was getting angry and walked away.

As expected the next morning I was ordered to attend the C.O's office, there were others in the queue waiting to see him, they were marched in one by one and stood to attention in front of his desk, some were there because they had been promoted and some because they were naughty boys and were awaiting punishment.

When it came to my turn, I was allowed to walk in at my own speed; I stood in front of the desk.

"Sargeant is it true that you are quite wealthy?" he asked.

"Yes, Sir, I'm a millionaire", I replied, knowing that he knew this already, someone in the top brass will have checked me out, and he had all the information he needed in front of him.

"Why did you join the army?" he asked, so I told him everything I had shouted at Rod the night before.

"And this is why you are having problems now, there will always be someone who is jealous and will have animosity against you, we cannot allow millionaires to be private soldiers, if you were an officer we may have allowed it, but according to your record you don't even want to be an NCO let alone an officer, so as from 8am this morning you are discharged from the army, here are your discharge papers" he said, handing me my red discharge book.

I didn't try to reason with him, I knew I was fighting a lost cause, so I just accepted my fate.

Back in the barrack room Rod was waiting for me.

"How'd it go?" he asked.

"As from 8am this morning I'm a civilian" I said.

"They've kicked you out, what you going to do now?" he asked.

"Go and live that millionaire life style that I should have been doing all along" I said.

"Private Sargeant" shouted Raggy Tash walking down the corridor to towards our room.

"Here" I shouted back.

"Private Sargeant don't forget to hand all your kit back in at the stores before you go" he said, putting his head around the door. By now I had changed into my civilian clothes and had packed my own personal gear.

"By the way Raggy, its Mister Sargeant to you and you can hand the fuckin kit in yourself, I'm off" I said,

"You've got to hand it in and get this chitty signed before they will give you your final pay" he stammered.

"Fuck the kit, fuck the chitty, fuck the pay and fuck the army", and with that I left the barracks got in my car and drove off the camp.

So that was it my life in the army was over and I suppose you're wondering what happened next.

Well I can tell you that.

Angela, didn't end up with six kids and a council house, no way, she got two kids, and a mansion house.

Oh! Yes, and me, I finally found the family I was looking for.

The kids are all grown up now and we have three little grandkids running around the place.

The only drawback is I've got Rod for a brother in law.

The End